Benin Folklore

Benin Folklore

Retold by *Funmi Osoba*

Illustrations by Tam Joseph

HADADA

For my mother and father

CONTENTS

Foreword

The writer of this volume of delightful folktales, Funmi Osoba, initially sent me three of them, "The Blind Man and the Lame Man", "The King who refused to Die" and " The Disobedient Child". I had intended to read them leisurely and at long intervals, one at a time. I read first "The Blind Man and the Lame Man". So enthralled was I by the story that I read the other two in quick succession, all at a sitting.

What I find fascinating about these tales is that they are entirely Nigerian in setting and spirit. They have no vestige of influence from any other culture. They exude Nigerian customs and traditions, and each story brings its cultural heritage into sharp focus.

The stories are set against the background of Nigerian landscape: the farmland with the maize fields and vegetable patches, the rocky scenery with large boulders, the rivers and streams where people fish and from where they fetch their daily supply of water. All are familiar scenes to Nigerians.

The seventeen stories in this volume are from Edo State, an area predominantly inhabited by the Binis, a fiercely proud people who are steeped in the beliefs of the powers of their oracles, divinations, the spirit world and of their ancestral gods. It is said that when reading historical chronicles of the

Binis, one reads a blend of fact and fiction. Funmi Osoba has employed this fusion cleverly in "The King who refused to die" and several other of the stories, bringing them alive in substance.

In the Nigerian Sunday Times of 23rd June, 1991, was published an article titled "Nigerian Folklore: Saving a Dying Heritage". I quote two extracts from the article:

1. *"After we have achieved a consensus for folklore as the main repository of history and values of the people, its erasure can only mean the extermination of the proofs of the heritage and history of the people."*

2. *"A fertile plot of land either grows crops when cultivated or weeds when discarded."*

These extracts are from the conclusion reached by the participants at a conference held at Ibadan by the Nigerian Folklore Society, a group dedicated to the preservation and promotion of the rich heritage of Nigerian folklore.

Folklore, in the context of the Ibadan conference, embraces sculpture, printing, drawing and all works of art, as well as writing, dancing and songs which depict events, scenes and characters, whether historical or fictitious, that are derived from Nigerian folktales.

I am aware of the scope and depth of research that Funmi Osoba undertook in order to produce these stories. Her hard work has indeed been rewarded, for she has not only presented some very interesting and most enjoyable tales, she has contributed in a great measure towards the ideals of the Nigerian Folklore Society.

Lady Ademola MBE OFA
Educationalist

Acknowledgements

I would like to thank Baba for his endless patience in narrating many of the legends over many, many hours. I would also like to thank Dr Aissen, Mrs Emily Obaseki, Dr Oni-Okpaku for his introductions and general assistance during the period when I was collecting the stories, Chief Inneh and Chief Omorodion Ogiaha.

Finally, I would like to thank those many people who, when asked, could only remember snippets of tales, which, when woven together, resulted in some of the stories retold in this compilation.

Folktales

The storytellers of old Africa are long since gone. These were men and women who had acquired a life time of wisdom. Their skill was not only in oratory, but also in drama and song. When they wove their stories, they could carry their audiences high above the clouds to take a peek at the gods or down below the seas to look into the grand palaces of the water goddesses. In their stories, they unravelled the language of animals and of all nature. In their stories, the world was young and new.

Today changes in Africa are occurring with startling speed. Few people have much interest in remembering the past. Frequently the old storytellers find they have no one to pass the stories on to, so they take the centuries of knowledge that they have acquired with them to the grave.

I hope this volume succeeds in preserving a few of the thousands of folktales which Africa once knew and loved so well.

Tortoise and
the Leopard

Tortoise was hungry. It was mid afternoon when he popped his head out of his shell and squinted at the fierce midday sun. "Goodness," he thought as he listened to his stomach rumble, "what wouldn't I do for a nice, delicious lunch?"

Tortoise looked up and saw Ibis the bird land on her nest high up in the branches of an iroko tree. She bent over her hungry children and began to feed them with a fat, juicy worm.

Tortoise then noticed that Spider had spun his web on a bush just ahead of him. The fly that was to be Spider's lunch wriggled helplessly in its sticky prison. Tortoise watched fascinated as Spider crawled towards his prey with slow, deliberate movements. Spider's long forearms stretched out towards the fly and yanked it loose. Tortoise continued to watch as Spider began to eat his lunch.

Tortoise now felt hungrier than ever. He picked himself up and went to look for someone who would give him something to eat. Soon he arrived at a market called Ekiogioso. This was a new market which had been opened recently. It was a place where all the animals could bring their crops to sell.

Now Tortoise was very lazy. All through the sowing season,

when the other animals had worked hard planting crops, Tortoise had not bothered to tend his farm. As a result, when the time came to harvest the crops, Tortoise had nothing because he had planted nothing.

Tortoise stood at the entrance to the market and looked around. A smile came over his face as he took in the delicious foods that were displayed for sale. There were masses of large, juicy fruit, piled high in baskets. There were huge mountains of cassava, beans, millet and maize. In fact, there was so much food that Tortoise's mouth began to water. He could see Antelope sitting by a fire, frying some akara balls. They gave off the most delicious aroma.

"Ah, my friend Antelope, I see you are well," Tortoise said as he sauntered up cheerfully.

Antelope knew how lazy and greedy Tortoise was. He nodded a silent greeting and used his ladle to turn over the akara balls which were now a golden brown. Tortoise stared at the food hungrily. Finally Antelope asked, "Would you like to buy some of my akara balls?"

Tortoise sighed heavily. "I would, Antelope, I would indeed, but I have no money. My crops did not ripen this year and I don't know how I will feed myself or my family."

Antelope had heard this story several times before. "I'm sorry, Tortoise," he said, though he did not feel in the least bit sorry for Tortoise, "But I can't help you. I need all the money I can get from the sale of my akara balls to buy food for my family."

Tortoise nodded sadly and moved off to the next stall. Goat was peeling the skins off cobs of maize before putting them on a grill to roast. The cobs were large and yellow. They looked extremely appetizing.

"Ah, my good friend Goat, how are you today?" Tortoise asked.

Goat looked up above the tops of his steel-rimmed glasses. "Thank you for asking, Tortoise. I am well," he replied in his thick, guttural voice.

"Then we must praise God," Tortoise replied, staring at the roasting cobs. "We cannot take good health for granted." He shook his head sadly and waited for Goat to inquire after his health. When Goat failed to respond, Tortoise added, "You know I've been ill, terribly ill...it's only God that said I should live, otherwise..." Tortoise shook his head again.

"I'm sorry to hear that," Goat replied shortly, but he was in no mood to be conned out of his produce, so he waited for Tortoise to ask for what he knew he had come for. Then he shook his head stubbornly. "My friend, you must learn to work as we all do. If you want some maize, you have to pay for it, like everybody else."

And so Tortoise left. He approached Hare, Snake, even grumpy old Owl, but the answers were all the same. No one was willing to give him anything for nothing.

Tortoise went back into the forest, disappointed and hungry. Hmmm! What a selfish bunch! he thought angrily. His mind was working overtime as he planned a way of getting even.

A few days later, Tortoise had decided on a plan. It was such a good plan, he thought, that he congratulated himself and would have given himself a pat on the back had his short hands been able to reach...

Tortoise knew that there were several entrances to the market. He carved an image of Leopard which he placed at one entrance behind a carefully arranged clump of grass. Next, Tortoise went to another corner of the market, and, disguising his voice, began to sing:

*Ekiogioso kpuma
nodogharie kpuma.*

Everyone was alarmed when they heard the song. The one creature animals and humans alike were afraid of was Leopard. A little boy screamed. He pointed to the leopard he could see at the entrance to the market. People looked - they could clearly see a leopard's face parting the bush. In a panic, everyone ran away in the opposite direction, instantly forgetting their wares. Within minutes, the market was deserted.

Tortoise waited. When he was sure that there was no one

around, he came out of his hiding-place and began to stuff food in his bag. Tortoise was greedy, and he stuffed so much food in the bag that he could barely carry it. Half-dragging and half-carrying the bag, he made his way to a safe place in the forest. There Tortoise made himself comfortable on a heap of dried leaves and began to stuff himself. He ate so much that he could not move afterwards, so he simply burped a few times and fell asleep, satisfied and happy.

The next day, Tortoise played his trick again. The stall-owners heard the song warning of Leopard's approach and they all ran, leaving their stalls unattended. The animals eventually returned to find their products ransacked as before. Quite understandably, they were upset. How long was this going to go on? they wondered.

A meeting of all the market-sellers was called and they debated what to do. Suddenly Dog came rushing into the meeting. He told all the animals to follow him and he took them to the entrance of the market. The animals were curious. What was it Dog wanted to show them? they wondered. They soon found out.

From its hiding-place behind the bushes, Dog pulled out the carved leopard. "This is what we have been running from," he said. The other animals looked at the leopard in amazement. From close up, the carving was so crude that it could not fool anybody, but from a distance it resembled the real thing and had fooled them all.

"Who could have pulled such a nasty trick?" asked Peacock.

"Who indeed?" Dog rubbed his head.

"We shall soon find out," Goat stated confidently.

All eyes turned to him. "You see, I have a plan," Goat continued.

The next day Tortoise arrived at the market to play his trick once more. He found his carved leopard where he had left it the previous day. Suspecting nothing untoward, he put it in position so that the animals would see its head parting the bushes. He then went to a corner of the market and started to sing, telling the animals that the leopard was approaching. Everyone ran away as they had done before. Soon, the market was deserted and Tortoise came out of his hiding-place.

Tortoise had grown in confidence and arrogance these past few days. What a bunch of stupid animals! he thought as he

began to fill his bag with food. Suddenly, from the corner of his eye, Tortoise saw a young boy standing at a stall. Angrily, he went up to the boy. He stood before him for a moment, but the boy just stared back. This made Tortoise angry. "Won't you run?" Tortoise said and, lashing out, he knocked the boy on the head.

To Tortoise's increasing annoyance, he found that his hand was stuck. To try and free it, Tortoise put his other hand on the boy's shoulder and pulled. To his dismay, his other hand was also stuck. Tortoise now kicked at the boy with his right foot, yelling, "Let me go! Let me go!" First his right foot and then his left foot stuck to the boy.

Tortoise suddenly realized that the boy had not moved once. He had continued to stand there, in exactly the same position with the same half-smile on his face. Tortoise looked closer and realized what he should have guessed all along. The boy was simply a painted wood carving, covered with an awful,

7

gooey, fast-drying glue. But this realization came too late. Tortoise was stuck.

Eventually, the animals came out of hiding. They saw Tortoise stuck to the wood carving, his half-full bag of food lying on the ground beside him.

The animals knew that they had caught their culprit. They beat Tortoise and left him stuck to the carving for several days. The animals jeered at him and the children made fun of him, jabbing him with sticks until he yelled.

When finally, several days later, Tortoise was released from his prison, he was hungry, exhausted and miserable. He crawled into the forest, having thoroughly learned his lesson.

The Blind Man and the Lame Man

Many, many full moons ago, there lived two friends. One was blind, the other was lame. Both men were miserably poor. They sat by the roadside begging all day in the hot sun. At first, the people who passed by took pity on the two men and dropped coins into their begging bowls. But, as the months wore on, the villagers got used to the sight of the blind man and the lame man. No longer did they feel much pity for them. Fewer and fewer coins were dropped into the little begging bowls. It reached a stage were at the end of the day the two friends had barely collected enough money to buy one plate of food.

One day, the two friends reached a decision. They would leave the village to look for somewhere better to live. "Surely," they reasoned, "Nowhere could be worse than this."

The blind man was strong, but he could not see. The lame man could not walk, but he was cunning. When the two travelled, the blind man would lift the lame man up onto his shoulders. The lame man would then guide the blind man. Several hours later, they reached a forest. The blind man was tired from carrying his lame friend all day, and his shoulders ached, so they decided to stop and rest for the night.

That evening, the blind man and the lame man set a few traps. They then went to bed, tired and hungry. The next morning, the two friends woke up at dawn, their stomachs rumbling from hunger. They went to examine their traps and, to their surprise, found that they had caught two large birds. The two friends could not believe their good fortune. They rejoiced, instantly forgetting their hunger and discomfort.

After washing, they made the long journey to the market. In no time, they had sold the birds for a good price. With the money they bought some food. There was change left over, and so they decided to buy a knife to help them cut sticks which could be used to make more traps.

The two friends arrived at their home and set several traps before retiring for the night. The next day they were amazed at their continuing good fortune when they found that every trap they had set now contained a large, juicy bird. The two friends could believe their luck. "At last, God is smiling on us," the lame man said.

"He must have heard our prayers," the blind man replied.

The two friends discussed their sudden good fortune and agreed that, since this place was good to them, they would remain awhile. It would not be difficult to build a house and cultivate a farm.

That day at the market things continued to go well. In no time the two friends sold all their game for a good price. With a large part of the money, they bought a machete. This they planned to use in clearing the land for their farm.

It was afternoon when the blind man took the lame man on his back and they went into the forest. After searching for a while, they found an old, disused farm where the undergrowth had not grown very thick. They spent the rest of the day clearing the bush. Actually, it was the blind man that did most of the work. The lame man had a rope tied around the blind man's waist. Complaining that he was to weak to work, the lame man sat by the edge of the farm and held onto the end of the rope. When it was time to go back to their camp, he simply tugged at the rope.

The blind man knew that he did most of the work, but did not mind. He had a kind heart and was very fond of his lame friend.

Day after day, they went to the farm. The blind man worked while the lame man talked. In this manner, the bush was burned and the land cleared. Finally, the land was ready for planting.

Now they needed seed to plant, so they set several traps. Luck was still on their side. All their traps were occupied the next day. With the game that was caught they could afford to buy plenty of good seed.

There was a large variety of seed on sale at the market. The lame man told the blind man what there was, describing the dozens of metal bowls piled high with lots of different types of seed including wheat, maize, millet and beans. The blind man thought a moment. He decided that maize would be the best seed to buy since this crop fetched the best prices. The lame man agreed. They went from stall to stall, inspecting the maize seed for sale. The blind man cautioned the lame man to be careful and buy a good grain of maize, one that would ripen quickly and was not diseased.

They bought the maize and planted it. Then they went home to rest. A week later, the two friends went out to the farm to see if the maize was sprouting. The blind man and the lame man stood on the edge of their farm. The lame man looked out at the farm which was now covered with little green shoots of maize. The blind man asked him what he saw. The lame man kept silent for a while. Then he said that there were no shoots to be seen. The blind man was disappointed. He said that perhaps they were too eager, perhaps they should give it more time. And so the two friends went back home.

A few days later the two friends went back to the farm. The lame man again deceived the blind man, saying that no shoots had yet come out of the ground. The blind man grew impatient. He turned to his friend and accused him of being careless and buying bad seed. The lame man denied the accusation, though he continued to deceive the blind man. The weeks passed and the maize grew sturdy and strong. The warm tropical sun ripened the cobs until, finally, they were ready for plucking.

The lame man realized that the maize could no longer be hidden. So he told the blind man that the shoots were now sprouting. The blind man decided to go and do some work on the farm to remove the weeds. The lame man told the blind man that he should hoe the ground carefully so as not to uproot the delicate shoots.

At the farm, the lame man tied the rope around the blind man's waist as usual. While the blind man was clearing the weeds, the lame man plucked a few cobs. He lit a fire and began to roast the cobs, whistling happily to himself. The blind man heard the crackling of the fire. He called out to his lame friend and asked what the noise was. The lame man shouted back, in between chewing mouthfuls of the juicy, succulent cobs, that it was nothing, probably just a falling stick.

The blind man could not see, but he could smell and hear. He could smell the delicious roasting cobs and knew the lame man was lying. But he said nothing. When the lame man had

eaten his fill, he put out the fire and pulled at the rope. The blind man put the lame man on his back and both went back home.

That night, the blind man told the lame man that he had reached a decision. "Life is far too cruel! Just look at us," he cried in exaggerated despair. "It has left us disabled, outcasts of society, people to be pitied and scorned. The maize we planted will not grow. Surely God has turned his back on us. Let us die," he went on, grabbing the lame man's arm, "Life is not worth living."

The lame man was concerned at the depth of emotion in the blind man's outburst. He listened to his friend, but his confusion kept him silent. He could not say, "I lied. The maize grew after all. God did not turn his back on us." So he kept silent.

They left their home together. The blind man carried the lame man and climbed to the top of a high hill. Down below, the ground was littered with sharp-edged rocks and stones. The blind man put his lame friend on the ground.

The lame man leaned forward and peered down the side of the hill at the rocks and stones below. He shivered and turned to the blind man. "My friend," he said, "As it was your idea, I suggest you jump first. I will follow."

The blind man would not hear of it. "Absolutely not!" he declared, "If I were to jump first, my good friend, what will happen if you are not able to get to the place from which to jump?" He knew the lame man planned to deceive him.

The lame man realized that the blind man was not going to allow himself to be tricked. So with a sigh he reluctantly agreed to jump first. After a warm and emotional goodbye in which the two friends hugged each other and cried a little, the lame man hobbled over to the side of the hill. He waited a few moments, then pushed a large stone over the edge. He watched as it tumbled into the abyss and crashed into the ground below. He then sat there quietly, not making a sound.

When the blind man heard the noise, he cried out, "Alas, my dear friend, before you went we should have cleared the bush here, so all might know that two friends had entered the spirit world from this place. Now I am alone, I must do the best I can." The blind man brought out his machete and began to cut the bushes and trees around him. He hit out wildly, striking everything that was in his path.

The lame man was sitting behind a bush which was directly in the blind man's path. He watched the blind man with increasing alarm. He tried to drag himself out of the blind man's path, but knew that he could not move fast enough. He wondered what he must do and, all the time, the blind man was getting closer and closer. The lame man looked up at the glint of the machete as it caught the reflection of the sun. He watched in horror as it struck the top of the bush behind which he was hiding. It was so close that, as the chopped grass flew into the air, it hit him in the face. The blind man raised the machete again. The lame man could bear it no longer. He cried out, "Wait!"

The blind man faked fury. He accused the lame man of being a cheat and a liar. Both men began to quarrel. Then, suddenly, God appeared out of the heavens. Both men were quiet as God told them to stop fighting. He told them that they had not been forgotten and that soon their lot would improve. The two men put aside their differences. The blind man carried the lame man and they went home.

The next day, they returned to the farm. The lame man told the blind man that some of the maize was now ripe and ready to eat. They lit a fire. The lame man picked some large, juicy cobs. He peeled off the skins and roasted them over the fire.

15

When the cobs were ready, he removed them from the fire and began to eat. The blind man sitting nearby could hear the lame man chewing the succulent cobs and he waited for his share. Finally, he realized that it was not forthcoming. He demanded that the lame man share the maize with him.

The lame man looked at the blind man who seemed so hungry and helpless. Smiling mischievously, the lame man picked up a frog and threw it onto the fire. When it was swollen and blackened, he removed it from the fire with a stick and handed it to the blind man, pretending that it was a cob.

The blind man received what he was given gratefully. Hungrily he bit into the belly of the frog. The frog burst open and its juices splashed into his face. The blind man screamed as liquid stung his eyes. The lame man watched as the blind man ran this way and that, all the time screaming in pain.

Suddenly the blind man stopped in his tracks. His eyes had stopped stinging. He stood still and rubbed his eyes, then slowly he opened them. Before him everything was a hazy mist. He blinked several times and, slowly, everything came into focus. He could see! He turned to see the lame man sitting by the fire holding a large, golden cob. Beyond was the farm he had laboured over for months. It was full of maize.

Overwhelmed by anger, the blind man picked up a stick and thrashed the lame man mercilessly. The lame man was terrified. Blows rained down on him. He begged the blind man to stop, but to no avail.

Suddenly, he could bear the pain no longer. He leapt up and ran off in his desperation to get away. A few seconds later he realized what he was doing. He stopped in his tracks and looked down at his once useless legs, now strong and healthy. "I can walk! I can walk!" he cried, jumping about wildly. He ran one way and then the other, all the time screaming hysterically.

God then spoke to the two men. To the blind man he said, "If the lame man had not given you a frog in deceit, you would never have gained your sight." To the lame man he said, "If the blind man had not beaten you in anger, you would never have walked. Go home and be friends - you both need each other."

The two men understood the wisdom of God's words. They made up their quarrel and went home. They quarrelled no more and prospered from their farm.

A Stranger's Gift

Along, long time ago, there lived a poor young man called Uwa, who decided to pay a visit to his relatives in a neighbouring village. As he was returning home one evening, Uwa saw a man lying by the roadside. At first he thought the man must be drunken tramp and decided to cross the road to avoid him, but, as he drew nearer, he heard the man's moans and cries.

"Help me...help me, please..." cried the man in a harsh whisper. Uwa stopped, unsure whether or not to cross the road and offer his help. But then, the thought occurred to him that it could be a clever trick. The man could be pretending to be in distress, hoping to fool people into coming close enough for him to rob them. Uwa had heard plenty of such stories and was justly cautious. He decided to continue on his way.

The man's cries got softer and softer, until they were barely audible, even though Uwa was now much closer. Then he saw the pool of blood that seeped out onto the road from where the stranger lay. Uwa instantly forgot his misgivings and rushed over.

"Help me...please," the stranger cried in a dull whisper, reaching out to Uwa.

Uwa took the injured man to his home which was a bare room in a clay hut. He bathed the stranger's wounds. Uwa had very little, but managed to beg food off neighbours from which he prepared delicious broth to feed his injured guest. He nursed the stranger as best he could. Soon the man began to show signs of recovery. When he could talk, he told Uwa how he came to be lying by the roadside. He had been going on a journey when armed robbers waylaid him, stole everything he had and beat him up badly, leaving him for dead. The stranger was immensely grateful to Uwa. He said that he had been lying by the roadside half-dead for several hours. Not one person who passed by had stopped to help him, until Uwa came along.

A few days later, the stranger was well enough to go home. He thanked Uwa profusely for his kindness and promised never to forget. Uwa watched the stranger hobble away on a makeshift crutch, thinking that was the last he would see or hear of him. The stranger stopped at the crossroads, waved goodbye one more time and then was gone.

Life in the village carried on as normal for Uwa. Each morning, he would take his hoe and machete to the farm. He would work all day on his small patch of land, trying to scratch a living from the dry, unproductive soil. The setting sun told Uwa that a day's work had been done. He was poor, pitifully poor. Most days, he could not afford the price of a plate of food. But he did not complain. Each day he tried to coax the land into giving him a better harvest than the year before.

One fine day, Uwa was working hard as usual on his farm, whistling merrily as he hoed a patch of land. He stood up to relieve the pressure on the muscles in his back and to wipe away the perspiration on his forehead. Suddenly, he sensed a presence. Uwa stopped whistling and squinted in the sun.

Then he saw a man standing in the distance. As he looked, the man raised a hand and waved in his direction. Uwa wondered who it could be - he was not expecting visitors. Holding his hoe in his left hand, he walked towards the visitor. Then Uwa recognized who it was. It was the robbery victim he had found lying by the roadside.

Uwa dropped his hoe and rushed over. The two exchanged hearty greetings. The stranger thanked Uwa several times for his kindness. He then gave the young farmer two things. One was a heavy little sack. The other, the stranger claimed, was a special gift. He told Uwa that he would come to recognize what it was at daybreak.

Uwa received the little sack gratefully. He bent to untie the string and discovered that it was filled with gold coins. Never before had he seen so much money. He looked up in amazement, but the stranger had disappeared...

For the first time ever, Uwa left the farm before the sun set. He went home thinking only of the stranger's gift. Entering his bare, bleak dwelling, he poured the contents of the sack onto his sleeping mat and gazed in wonder at the pile of gold coins. He picked one up and let it rest in the palm of his hand. The value of just one little gold coin was far greater than a whole year's harvest, he thought. Uwa smiled; then he laughed out loud, long and hard. The realization began to sink in that he was now a rich man.

Years passed. Uwa used his money wisely and he became very wealthy. He was able to live in a big house. He now had a wife and several children. Uwa was content with life.

Before we go on, I would like to take you back. Remember the stranger had mentioned a special gift?

The night after Uwa had received the gold coins, he was

sleeping on his mat, dreaming happily of his unexpected wealth. Suddenly he heard a voice say, "The witches of the night are leaving. It is safe to wake up now." Uwa's eyes sprang open. He sat up on his bed. What on earth was that? he wondered. But there was silence. It was still pitch-black outside, so, after a few minutes, he thought he must have been dreaming. He lay down on his mat and, before long, was fast asleep once more.

Soon the early morning rays filtered through the wooden shutters of the room. Uwa shifted on his mat, but he was still sleeping peacefully when a voice cut through his subconscious. "Wake up, wake up!" it shrilled, "The day has begun. Wake up, wake up!"

Uwa's eyes sprang open. Who on earth was that? he wondered, thinking what a peculiar-sounding voice it was too. Never had he heard anything like it. He lay there for a moment, eyes open, wondering whether to get up and investigate, when it sounded again, "Wake up! Begin your day! Wake up!"

Uwa froze. Suddenly he knew exactly what he was hearing. It was the cock crowing. But instead of hearing the familiar "Cock-a-rooooo-cooo", Uwa realized that he could now understand exactly what the bird was saying. Uwa knew then what his special gift was. He could understand the language of animals.

Suddenly he shivered, for the knowledge gave him a wierd, uncomfortable feeling. He wondered what to do. Then he remembered the stranger's words, "Tell no one about your special gift or you will lose it instantly."

And so the years passed. Uwa kept the knowledge of his

special gift to himself. He told no one, not even his wife or children.

One evening, Uwa was sitting in the back porch of his large house, watching the setting sun cast its orangey glow on the horizon. He watched the farmhands lead the ox to the barn standing to his left. The evening breezes were cool and gentle. Uwa liked nothing better than to take a stroll through his land. This was the perfect time. Soon night would fall, the darkness covering the world with a velvety cloak, broken only by the twinkling of a thousand stars. Now he could see the farmhands lock the barn door. Uwa got up to begin his walk.

As he passed by the barn he heard the ox complaining to the donkey. Uwa decided to stop and listen.

Ox said, in between chewing mouthfuls of succulent grass, "How could they work an animal so hard? Do these humans have no sympathy in their hearts? They flog me as if I were a log of wood. Sometimes I wish I could make them understand that it hurts me just as much as it would hurt them."

Donkey grunted a reply, more out of politeness than anything. He had to listen to Ox's complaints every evening, and he was bored.

Ox continued, "Ah, but you are so lucky, Donkey."

Donkey looked up. "Why?" he queried.

"They never flog you - you can do what you want with your days. All you have to do is take Master to the market once a week. I wish I were as lucky as you." Ox bent his head and finished off the pile of grass that was his supper.

Donkey watched Ox for a few moments in disgust. "You know what your problem is - you are greedy. That is why they work you so hard."

"But...but..." Ox began, confused.

Donkey cut in. "Look, let me give you a bit of advice my

friend. Do not be so eager to gobble up all your food. I know that if you refuse your food today and tomorrow, then roll over on your back and start spitting and groaning the next day, they will be so worried that they will call the vet. You kick him out in a spasm of agony. Then they will realize you are seriously ill and will not take you to the farm."

Ox considered what Donkey said for a moment. "Do you really think it will work?" he asked cautiously.

"But of course," Donkey replied arrogantly, "I know humans. They are not very difficult animals to understand. Do as I say and I bet you will not have to work for the next few days."

At this point, Uwa decided he had heard enough. Cutting his walk short, he went back to the house.

The next evening, Ox was brought back from the farm at sunset as usual. A huge bale of hay was placed before him and fresh water poured into his drinking bowl. Ox watched the farmhands retire for the night before looking at his supper. His back ached from the flogging he had received that day, and he was tired and hungry, but all day he had thought of nothing else but Donkey's advice. He had come to the decision that it was worth trying. With enormous will-power, he ignored his rumbling stomach, walked over to his corner of the barn and lay down to sleep.

In the morning the farmhands returned. They saw the ox's uneaten supper and became immediately concerned. They made straight for the house to report it to their master.

Uwa listened as the farmhands reported their concern. Even though he knew exactly what was going on, he did not let on. Instead, he pretended to be concerned. Then he said, "Feed him again this evening and let me know if he still refuses his food."

The next morning, the farmhands came to report that the ox

had once again refused the food. He had not even drunk the water in his bowl. The farmhands were now even more worried. "It could be he is ill," they suggested to the master, "This has never happened before."

Uwa nodded understandingly. "Yes, quite possibly," he agreed, "But before we call the vet, let's try one more time. Give him the best hay you can find."

And so the farmhands went away. But as they placed the fresh hay in front of Ox, it suddenly started to grunt and groan in a most peculiar manner. Then it rolled over onto its back and began foaming at the mouth. The farmhands rushed out of the barn, alarmed. Never had they seen anything like this.

The vet was summoned. He came with his bag of medicines. Ox was still grunting and groaning and foaming at the mouth as the elderly gentleman entered the barn. He took one look at the animal and shook his head. This does not look good, he thought. He went closer to the animal to try and examine it, but Ox suddenly appeared to be in a hysterical frenzy. It rolled about on its back, spitting and foaming, legs flailing wildly in

the air. A hind leg caught the vet in the small of the back, flinging him out of the barn.

The farmhands rushed to the vet, helping him up and dusting off his clothes. "Are you all right?" they asked.

The vet nodded. He reported his findings to Uwa. "I think you have a very sick animal there," he began gravely, "He is verrrry, verrrrry ill indeed."

"We must make sure he gets better then," Uwa said.

"Quite right. Give him lots of food and water, and complete, I stress, *complete* rest for at least a week."

Ox was made comfortable and allowed to rest. But the next day the farmhands went to Uwa with a problem.

"Sir," they said, "we need an ox to pull the plough or we will not be able to plough the land."

Uwa was prepared for this. Without a moment's hesitation, he said, "Put the plough on the donkey."

For a moment, the farmhands were not sure they had heard right. "Sir?" they said.

"You heard," retorted Uwa, "Put the plough on the donkey. Let him work for a change. He is a lazy animal. What does he do except carry me to the market once a week? Let donkey do some work for a change - hard work never hurt anyone."

And so a surprised donkey was led out of the barn. As the farmhands began to put on his back the heavy yoke that would later be attached to the plough, Donkey realized in alarm what was going to happen. He began to protest. But his neighs and grunts were ignored. Donkey was led to the farm.

And so the day passed. Donkey, who had only known a life of ease and contentment, was made to pull the heavy plough first this way and then that under the blazing sun. When he tried to rest for a few moments, he was flogged mercilessly and made to return immediately to work.

Meanwhile, Ox whiled the hours away sleeping and eating in the shade of the barn. This is the life, Ox thought contentedly, whisking his tail lazily to get rid of a fly playing on his back. He was half-asleep when they brought Donkey back into the barn.

Donkey groaned and grunted with agony. "Look at my back," he complained to Ox. "Never before have I been so mistreated..." He felt so sorry for himself.

Ox listened while smiling contentedly. A thought occurred to him - he wondered how he had never before noticed the scent of the hay. It was a sweet, soft smell which was making him drowsy. Then he remembered Donkey was talking. "Ehnn?" he asked.

Donkey looked at Ox annoyed. "I said *you* will have to work tomorrow."

"And give up all this? You must be joking," Ox replied, shocked. Donkey looked at Ox in alarm. "But you've had your rest, and the plan was not for me to take your place."

"Well, get used to it."

"What do you mean?" Donkey asked, not liking the sound of what he was hearing, nor Ox's ungrateful attitude.

"I did not know how great your life was, Donkey. I think I will be ill for a long time, a long, *long* time." Ox promptly closed his eyes and went to sleep.

Donkey watched Ox with a mixture of alarm and anger. "Selfish beast!" he muttered angrily, thinking what a great, big, useless, ungrateful animal Ox was.

Each day for the rest of the week, the farmhands would come at the crack of dawn to lead Donkey out of the barn to begin work on the farm. As he suffered under the heat of the sun, pulling the plough which got heavier and heavier as the

day wore on, Donkey knew he had to find a way to get Ox back to work.

Meanwhile, Ox was putting on weight daily. His food portions had been doubled morning, noon and evening. With nothing to do all day but laze around. Ox had by now almost forgotten what it was like to work in the farm, to pull the plough first this way and then that. To be flogged mercilessly by the farmhands whom he could never please.

That evening as Donkey was brought back from the farm, Ox watched him from the corner of his eye, waiting for the usual complaints. Uwa was standing behind the barn door waiting to hear the animals conversation as he had done every evening since overhearing Donkey's initial advice to Ox.

Unaware of Uwa's presence, Ox had been busy thinking how to get the master to build him a larger barn, something more spacious. Should he kick down this one? he was wondering as he waited for Donkey to tell him what hell it was working on the farm.

But to Ox's surprise there were no complaints from Donkey. In fact, Donkey silently ate his supper and curled up to sleep.

27

Ox could not stand the silence any longer. "Ehnnnn..." he coughed. Donkey ignored him. After a while, Ox's curiosity got the better of him, so he asked, "Donkey, how was work?"

Donkey shrugged, not bothering to open his eyes.

"Didn't they beat you?"

"I'm not complaining. In fact, I thank God for allowing me to work."

Now Ox was more than curious. A lazy animal like Donkey, grateful for being made to work hard, now he had heard everything. "What do you mean?" he asked.

"It's just that I heard something the farmhands said today which made me praise God, but it is nothing..."

"Nothing? What did they say?" Ox demanded.

Donkey rose and came over. Affecting an expression of deep concern, he said, "Ox, it is only because I am your friend that I will tell you. Somebody else would just keep it to themselves."

"Yes, go on, go on, " Ox retorted impatiently.

"Well, it was like this," Donkey began, "I heard Master and one of the farmhands talking. When I realized they were discussing you, I decided to listen."

"What did they say?" Ox asked, alarm creeping in cold shivers down his spine.

"They said that since your illness you have become so useless. All you do is eat and sleep and get fat. Since you don't do any work, there is no point in keeping you."

"What are they planning to do?" Ox asked, fear making his voice a high-pitched whisper.

"They are sending you to the butcher's."

"Whatttt!!!!!" screeched Ox.

Donkey nodded, sadly. "Tomorrow."

"But how can they...me...*me*, the strongest and most useful animal on the farm? Have they forgotten already?"

"You know how fickle these humans are," Donkey replied disgustedly. "Never mind, Ox, I will always remember what a good friend you were."

"I must show them." Ox said, suddenly reaching a decision. "Tomorrow I will show them that I am still the most hard-working animal on the farm."

At this point, Uwa decided to go back indoors. But what he had heard so amused him that he began to laugh. And when he started he could not stop. He laughed so much that he almost split his sides. His wife had never seen him laugh so hard. She wanted to know what was so funny.

"Nothing," Uwa told her unconvincingly, for he still continued to laugh.

His wife watched him laugh. Spasms racking his body, tears flowing freely down his cheeks. She was now more curious than she had ever been about anything, so she pestered him all night, crying, begging, pleading. "A good husband keeps no secrets from his wife," she urged.

Finally, Uwa sat her down, knowing that he would forever lose his special gift as he began to tell her the story of the injured stranger....

Spider and the Antelope

There once lived a man who decided to farm. He went out into the bush and chose a place that was suitable. He felled the trees and went home. As it was the rainy season, he realized that now was not a good time to light a fire to clear the bush. And so he waited for the dry season to come when he could clear his farm.

One day, Spider happened to find the land. He decided that this was a good place to settle. Spider began to spin his web. Soon his family increased. The land was peaceful and food was plentiful. Spider and his family lived contentedly, unaware of the impending danger.

Antelope also wandered onto the land. He too felt that it was a good place to live. The land was fertile. A nearby stream provided a plentiful supply of fresh water. There was peace and calm, and none of the human predators in sight. Antelope also brought his family. And so it happened that both Spider and Antelope made this land their home.

The months passed by. The rains grew less and less until, one day, the dry season arrived. The farmer came out to prepare his farm. He arrived at the bush and made a pile of sticks to light a fire.

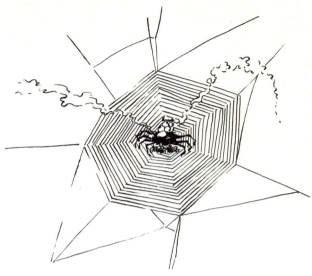

Spider had just finished a hearty meal of a delicious butterfly and was lounging contentedly on a leaf when he first became aware that something was not quite right. He opened his eyes and listened. The vibrations he picked up through the hairs on his body told him there was an unusual presence around. He lifted himself up on his leaf and looked out into the bush. His large eyes gave him an extremely wide field of vision, but he could see nothing untoward. The grasshopper that he was planning to have for lunch was dancing merrily in the sun. Spider looked at it for a moment. Then he turned, twisting his body. The wind whistled through the bush, swaying the lilies.

Antelope was munching contentedly on some leaves. A flock of birds swooped low overhead as they prepared to land on the stream. Everything seemed normal. Spider listened a moment longer. Then he yawned, leaned back on his leaf and fell asleep.

Meanwhile, the farmer had finished collecting enough

dried sticks and moss to light a fire. He threw some kerosene over the heap and set fire to it. The fire spread quickly, helped by the dryness of the land and the wind. Before anyone knew what was happening, it had spread wildly through the bush. Now suddenly where there had once been peace and contentment, the farmer had brought chaos and destruction.

Antelope and his family had strong, fast legs that could carry them quickly out of danger. Antelope cried to his family to follow him and they prepared to race away from the fire, through the bush. Spider heard the pandemonium. At first he thought it was only a dream, but then he was unceremoniously knocked off his leaf as a young antelope sped past. Spider woke up properly, startled and annoyed. "What on earth...?" he began, then stopped. Everywhere he saw animals racing away from the danger. Moments later he saw the fire savagely scarring the land. It was dangerously close. He huddled his family together and wondered what to do. He knew that his legs were not fast enough to carry him away from the danger. Then he saw Antelope prancing impatiently on nimble legs, waiting to make sure that every member of his family got away safely. Spider called out to him, "Antelope !"

Antelope looked down at Spider. Spider called out desperately, "Antelope, please help my family and me, otherwise we shall perish in the fire."

The fire was now very close, so close that the heat and smoke filled the air. Antelope was not interested in what Spider had to say. Saving his own life was far more important. He moved away. Spider called out, even more desperately now, "Please, Antelope, dear friend, *please* help us. I promise I will repay your kindness some day."

Antelope turned and looked down at Spider. "You?" he

asked curiously, "But you are only a spider. What could you possibly do to help me?"

Spider continued to beg Antelope. Antelope was not a selfish person. He looked at the fire which was spreading rapidly. He knew that if he left, Spider and his family would perish. So he lowered his head and allowed Spider and his family to clamber on his back. "Hurry up! Hurry up!" Antelope urged as the fire got closer and closer. When Spider and his family were all safely clinging to his back, Antelope darted through the bush away from the fire.

Eventually, they arrived at a safe place. No longer could they smell the smoke of the fire. The air was fresh once again. Antelope lowered his head gently. Spider and his family climbed down and they thanked Antelope for saving their lives.

Time passed. Spider found a place to set up a new home. Life slowly returned to normal. Antelope also happened to set up his new home quite close by.

Not too far was a pathway leading to a village. Now the animals have a law which says that animals are not allowed to cross manmade paths because of the threat from the human predators. One day, Antelope was in a haste to get home. He absent-mindedly crossed the path, leaving his footprints in the soft earth. Not long afterwards, a hunter came by. He saw the fresh footprints and knew that an antelope was nearby. The hunter hurried home to get his gun.

Hidden by the bush, Antelope watched the hunter, alarmed. He wondered what he should do. Spider saw Antelope looking very worried and asked what the matter was. Antelope told Spider about his careless mistake in crossing the path.

Spider thought for a moment. then he said, "You saved my life once, now I will save yours."

He told Antelope to hide behind a tree. Then Spider brought out all his family. They gathered on the path and began to weave their web. They spun and spun and spun. The web grew larger and larger and larger. It was so large that it covered all of Antelope's tracks.

The hunter returned with his gun, eager to start tracking Antelope. He reached the spot where he thought he had seen the footprints, but could not understand why all he saw was a spider's web. He searched the path for the footprints, but could not find any. The hunter scratched his head, confused. He had no footprints to start tracking, so what was he to do? The animals in the bush kept very quiet as they watched the hunter stare at the ground in frustration. Finally, he admitted defeat and went home.

Antelope then came out of hiding and thanked his little friend Spider for repaying his debt and saving his life.

Revenge of the River Goddess

Igbaghon was once a human being like you or me. She lived in a small, quiet village with her parents and did all the things young girls did. Sometimes she was tiresome, but she could also be extremely charming.

As Igbaghon grew older, her parents began to notice something unusual about their child. It was nothing they could ever put their fingers on, but she had a strange defiant spark in her eyes that was most unsettling. She was always asking the strangest questions and perplexing her poor old parents. Her mother muttered often enough, "That child is cleverer than she has any right to be." And she meant it too. Igbaghon's parents were simple folk, living a simple life. In their peasants' life of toil and grind there was no room for unnecessary questions. All the mother ever wanted was for her daughter to settle down with a nice man and raise a family.

As the years passed, Igbaghon's mother grew increasingly alarmed. It did not look as if her daughter would ever get married. Her fiercely independent spirit put off suitors. Men did not want wives who told them what to do. Women were expected to keep their mouths shut and know their place.

Eventually Igbaghon's parents decided that enough was

enough. Something had to be done about their daughter. All
the girls her age were married and having children - why
should their daughter be any different? So these two simple
folk went looking for a husband for Igbaghon. They found the
Enogie. He lived in a grand palace with several servants and
wives to attend to his every need.

Now it is true that Igbaghon was a peasant's daughter. How
she came to be given in marriage to a titled chief as grand as the
Enogie will probably never be known. But this is what
happened and so the story continues.

You might have thought that, because Igbaghon's future
husband was a wealthy man, she was a lucky young woman on
her way to a life of privilege and luxury. But this was not to be
the case...

The Enogie had a reputation, and not a very good one. He
was well known for collecting wives the way others collected
clothes, and for discarding them in a similar manner. There
were rumours about some of the awful things he did to his
wives, but Igbaghon's parents shrugged off the warnings of
friends. They were desperate to get their daughter married
and off their hands. Already she had reached an age when
people were talking.

So, early one morning, Igbaghon packed her dearest
possessions, said an emotional goodbye to her parents, for she
knew that she would never see them again and set off on the
journey that would take her to the village of her husband-to-
be.

It did not take Igbaghon long to realize what sort of man her
husband was. He was mean, nasty and egotistic. Igbaghon had
no intention of behaving like his other dutiful wives, scrambling
for the morsels of attention he tossed their way, or bickering
like fishwives. She did not bother making friends with the

other women because she knew they would never understand her. She much preferred her own company. Soon she had acquainted herself with her new environment, exploring the forest by day and night. When she needed friends, the animals were there for her. And for a while, Igbaghon was content.

There were very few people who knew exactly how many wives the Enogie had. The Enogie was not one of them. He had almost forgotten he had taken Igbaghon as a wife when one day he happened to see her entering the palace grounds. "Who is that?" he asked his attendants, and was not a little surprised when he was told. From then on he took a special interest in Igbaghon. He noticed at once she preferred to keep to herself instead of mixing with the other women. He noticed also that there was something strange about her, something he could never quite put his finger on. Even though he would never admit it, there was something about her that made him uneasy. Was it the defiant spark that burned in her eyes when he insulted her, or was it something else? What was it exactly he often wondered? The Enogie did not know, but one thing he was sure about was that whatever it was he did not like it.

The Enogie was a man who was used to being in control. When he wanted something, it was a brave person that dared refuse. The Enogie decided that what he wanted was to remove the defiant spark that shone so brightly in Igbaghon's eyes. Then, he believed, she would be passive and submissive like his other wives. So he beat and bullied her unrelentingly. Daily, he dreamed of numerous ways of humiliating her. It gave him pleasure to abuse her in front of strangers and children. He would watch her cower, but still the strange, defiant spark remained in her eyes.

Never one to admit defeat, this desperately unpleasant man encouraged all his children, especially his eldest son,

Emokpagbe, whom he adored, to mock and bully Igbaghon. He hoped that they would succeed where he had not. But they did not, for nothing ruffled Igbaghon.

Finally, with particularly malicious glee, the Enogie decided to ban Igbaghon from leaving the palace and thereby cutting off her final link with the outside world. He fervently hoped that this would subdue her. But, after a few weeks, the Enogie again realized that his latest plan had failed, for Igbaghon was still as defiant as ever.

Igbaghon refused to obey her husband's orders. She would sneak out of the palace under the cover of darkness to enjoy her long, peaceful walks in the forest and her conversations with the creatures of the woods.

One day, Igbaghon was returning from one of her forbidden visits. She sneaked into the palace and down the main corridor which would take her to her room. As she crept along the passageway, she saw a light from her husband's sitting-room. Realizing he was still awake, she removed her sandals and prepared to steal past the door.

Sounds of laughter reverberated through the walls. Igbaghon realized that the Enogie had company. She tiptoed past the partially shut door and had gone few feet when she stopped. She crept back to the door and listened. Igbaghon was sure she had heard her name.

Through the crack in the door she could see that there were three other men in the room besides her husband. The men were older, much older than her husband. She watched them for a few moments before realizing that they were priests. As she stood behind the door listening to the conversation in the other room, she suddenly became more frightened than she had ever been in her whole life.

The Enogie was discussing a festival to honour his ancestors. This festival was a grand affair which was performed once a year. Apparently this year's celebrations would be special because the Enogie was planning to sacrifice to his ancestors not just the usual cows and goats. He had called the priests to discuss the human sacrifice he had decided to make. The sacrificial victim would be none other than Igbaghon.

Instinct told Igbaghon to run, make for the forests and run. But she knew that she would be caught eventually and returned to her husband. There was nowhere for her to go. She could not return to her parents' home. A wife who left her husbands' home, whatever the circumstances, was considered to have brought shame and disgrace on the family.

Igbaghon returned to her room. As she sat on the bed staring through a window at the full moon, she prayed to her ancestors. Silently, she begged them to help her.

The ancestors must have heard her, for then, a miracle

happened. A cloud floated by, obscuring the face of the moon for a moment, and in that instant the transformation happened. Igbaghon became an eagle. The proud, majestic bird sat on the window-sill for a few moments. Then she squeezed herself out through the iron bars, spread her wings and flew away...

As Igbaghon flew deeper and deeper into the forests, soaring over the treetops, she did not once look back. Her silent resolve was that, if she ever came across anything belonging to the Enogie, she would destroy it, utterly.

Dawn was breaking when Igbaghon got to a place she thought she could make her home. She swooped towards the ground. As soon as her claws touched the earth, a mighty river was formed. Igbaghon entered the water and became immortal...

Igbaghon ruled in the underworld below the waters. She was the goddess of the river. In her magnificent palace she had great wealth and numerous servants. But, even though Igbaghon was now free from the tyranny of her husband to live the life of luxury and peace she had always dreamed of, she still harboured a deep hatred for all human beings. She kept her promise to destroy any who dared to trespass on her territory. So people who came to the banks of the river to fetch water or bathe never returned to their homes. As years went by, the river gained a fearful reputation. People stopped using its waters. No one even dared venture within sight of it. At night, wise old men would narrate stories to the young about the powerful, unsettled spirit of the river who refused to be pacified with sacrifices or gifts.

One day, Igbaghon was playing with her maids when a servant came rushing up to her. "What is it?" she asked impatiently. She was winning at the game of Ayo, and she did not want to be disturbed.

"My Lady," the maid said urgently, "a young mortal man sits by the river, washing his feet in your waters."

At this, Igbaghon immediately lost interest in the game. She turned to the maid. "Can this be true?" she cried, frowning in annoyance. The young girl nodded meekly. Igbaghon got up suddenly, pushing her maids out of the way. She swam through her palace and up to the surface of the waters.

The clear waters parted as Igbaghon rose to the top. She remained still for a moment as she took in her surroundings. It had been so long since she had come up to the world of mortals that everything seemed new and a little strange. The dense forests bordering the banks were encroaching on her domain, their roots practically growing in her waters. I must speak to the tree spirit about that, Igbaghon thought fleetingly. It was a fine day, and the skies were blue. But the sun shone so fiercely that it hurt her eyes. Igbaghon looked away quickly, and then she saw him.

It was true. A young man sat on a rock by the bank of the river. He had removed his sandals and was dabbling his feet in the water. Anger immediately welled up inside Igbaghon. How dare he? she thought. Has he not heard of my powers?

The trespasser was not aware of Igbaghon's presence nor that of her hand-maidens some distance away. He seemed preoccupied with his own private thoughts as he continued to stare down into the river, letting the clear, refreshing waters bathe his feet.

As Igbaghon neared the young man, she suddenly recognized him. He was Emokpagbe, her husband's eldest son. Now I will have revenge, she thought as she silently slipped out onto the

bank and ran up to Emokpagbe. Before he knew what was happening, she had grabbed hold of his arm in an iron grip.

Emokpagbe looked up, startled, then amazed and humbled by the radiant figure clothed in coral beads that stood before him. The defiant spark that shone in her eyes seemed to burn through him.

"So you have come to taunt me?" Igbaghon cried angrily. "Have you not heard of what happens to trespassers, or are you merely a brave fool?"

Emokpagbe stood up slowly, taking in Igbaghon's impressive presence. It occurred to him that something about her was familiar, and he wondered where he could have been so fortunate to have met such a majestic and impressive figure of a woman.

"I don't understand...I didn't mean to trespass," he said politely, "but I've been travelling for days. I do not know these parts well."

Igbaghon stared up at Emokpagbe. "So you do not know who I am?" she said slowly, a hard smile creasing her face.

"I'm sure I would have remembered if I had had the pleasure of meeting you," Emokpagbe replied, all sweetness and charm. "Could you let go of my arm," he continued, "It's hurting..."

"Look closer," Igbaghon said, squeezing the arm tighter and bringing her face nearer to his.

Puzzled, Emokpagbe suddenly realized that they had an audience. Numerous mermaids sat on the rocks dotted around the banks of the river, watching in silence. He was extremely uneasy as he allowed himself to stare into Igbaghon's face. It was a handsome face, but her skin was the strangest he had ever seen, covered as it was with tiny, translucent scales. The defiant eyes stared hard at Emokpagbe, and guiltily he took his eyes away.

"How is your father?" she asked softly.

Emokpagbe suddenly felt as if he had been slapped, cold and hard. Now he remembered.

"Y..y..y..you are..." he stammered.

"Yes, now you know who I am. Take a moment. Look around you," Igbaghon sneered, pointing to the mermaids who surrounded them, and the vast expanse of river beyond. "All this is mine. How does it compare with your father's miserable palace?"

"Please let me go. I promise never to come this way again," Emokpagbe began to beg.

"Why should I show you any mercy? When you used to make fun of me? When you put snakes in my bed or bugs in my food, did you ever show me any mercy?"

"It was a long time ago. I did not mean it, any of it. I was only a child then. I am sorry, desperately sorry. I would do anything now to make it up to you. If I told Baba, I'm sure he would be happy to give you whatever you asked for, or I could..."

"That old fool," Igbaghon spat, cutting him short, "What could he give me that I do not already own?" She paused to think for a moment. "But if my memory serves me well," she continued, "you were the most precious thing in his life. To destroy you would be revenge enough for me."

The hand-maidens saw the anger in their mistress and rushed up to her to plead for the young man's life. Igbaghon listened to their cries of mercy. Eventually, she turned to Emokpagbe and told him to be thankful that his life was saved. The young man knelt down to thank her, but no words came from his mouth. Igbaghon re-entered the water. The last thing Emokpagbe heard as she disappeared below the surface of the river, never to be seen again, was her laugh. It rang through the forest like a thousand tinkling bells...

Igbaghon was satisfied. In making Emokpagbe dumb, she had at last got her revenge. Never again did she return to the surface of the water. Never again did she punish any human who strayed into her domain. She returned to her land of immortality. And the river continues to bear her name to this day.

Emokpagbe's Cure

In the story, "Revenge of the River Goddess" we saw how Emokpagbe was struck dumb by his avenging stepmother, Igbaghon. Emokpagbe wandered through the forest for several days, confused and disorientated. Eventually, he found his way home. The people could not believe that this gibbering, babbling wreck was the proud young man who had left the town a few weeks earlier. No one could understand what had happened to him. When Emokpagbe tried to speak, the only sounds that would come out of his mouth were grunts and forced, unintelligible, high-pitched croaks. He was unsteady on his feet and barely had control of his muscles, lapsing into uncontrollable shaking fits.

Days passed and Emokpagbe's condition still had not improved, to the increasing worry of his father, the Enogie. Word was sent out. The Enogie was determined to find someone to cure his son's condition. No cost was spared. Daily, an endless stream of juju priests, herbalists, faith healers and physicians filed through the palace. Each offered some new miraculous cure. Each was confident that they had the remedy for Emokpagbe's condition.

The Enogie was desperate to try anything to cure his son.

He would listen to the promises of obscure miracle-workers and allow his hopes to be raised. But their failures pushed him lower down the dark tunnel of despair. For the first time in his life, the Enogie felt completely out of control. He became increasingly dispirited. Stress etched deep lines in his face. His hair turned grey with worry. His eyes paled with sadness. He lost weight as he lost hope. Anxiety had made him less than a shadow of his former self.

A long way away, in an obscure village, approached only after crossing seven forests and seven rivers, there was said to live a man who was fast gaining a reputation as an extraordinary physician well versed in the secrets of the supernatural. This man was the Chief of Obo. His powers inspired fear and deep respect among all those who came across him.

One day, Emokpolo, who was Emokpagbe's mother, approached her husband the Enogie with news of the Chief of Obo. Word had come to her about his powers and, after hearing about some of his deeds, she was justly impressed. She rushed to tell her husband of what she had heard. The Enogie sat cross-legged on a mat in a corner of his room, muttering silent words of prayer. Emokpolo could not be sure if he had heard a word she had said, for not once did he look at her. As she knelt before her husband, it dawned on her just how much he had changed since Emokpagbe's illness. She took in his skinny, wasted limbs, his red-rimmed eyes sunken deep in their sockets, his grey, scraggly beard which made him look so old and weak. It surprised Emokpolo that she had ever been afraid of this man. The Enogie barely seemed to be aware of his wife's presence. Slowly she stood up and left the room.

Emokpolo was determined to protect her son's inheritance. Since a dumb person could not be a ruler, that meant finding a cure, no matter the cost. So she made the decision to make the terrifying journey to the land of the Chief of Obo. Somehow she knew that he was their last hope.

At the break of dawn Emokpolo set off with Emokpagbe on the long journey that would take them across seven forests and seven rivers to the land of the Chief of Obo. They made a strange sight. To fend off trouble, Emokpolo draped herself in rags and an odd assortment of clothes. She knew that people usually left alone those who were considered insane. Emokpagbe was dressed similarly, his jerking movements only serving to convince those people they came across that these were indeed two poor, mad people.

The journey was long and slow. After seven weeks, they reached the seventh forest. This forest was quite unlike any of the others that they had crossed. Its strange, ominous atmosphere was augmented by the absence of any living creatures. No birds called out to one another, no bush rats scrambled for food in the dense undergrowth, there were no antelopes or squirrels, no snakes slithered in the dirt, no flies danced around the travellers' faces. And as if that were not unsettling enough, Emokpolo noticed that the forest also had the strangest trees she had ever seen. They were tall and gnarled, and seemed to watch the strangers like jealous wives.

As they went deeper, the forest grew denser and denser as if closing up to form an impenetrable barrier. Eventually, the forest was so thick that the tops of the trees completely shut out the sunlight. Emokpolo knew she was close to the land of Obo. But her machete was no match for the thick, dense, thorny bush. When night fell, she made a bed of leaves for her son and sat beside him. Soon he fell asleep. Emokpolo looked around at the strange, mysterious forest. The night was dark. All around she could hear strange whispers and feel invisible eyes watching her. But fear no longer had any meaning for Emokpolo.

Exhaustion overcame her and she fell asleep. She dreamed she was surrounded by spirits. Some carried her on their shoulders, others parted the bushes. Then she dreamed she was sitting before the Chief of Obo. She felt somebody shake her hand gently. Emokpolo opened her eyes and saw Emokpagbe kneeling before her.

"What is it?" she cried in a sudden panic.

Emokpagbe pointed to the bushes, a smile on his face. Emokpolo stood up and looked on in amazement. Bushes and trees alike were bent almost double to expose a path. It was as if a pair of large invisible hands were holding the forest apart, inviting them to continue on their journey. A miracle had indeed happened. Emokpolo and Emokpagbe picked up their possessions and entered the deepest part of the forest. As they walked, the bushes before them continued to be mysteriously pulled apart, leaving the bushes behind them to close in again.

Several days later, they had crossed the forest. And the invisible hand disappeared as mysteriously as it had come.

Soon they began to pass settlements. Villagers took in the two strangers and their bizarre appearance. From the way the villagers stared and whispered amongst themselves, Emokpolo got the impression that they had been expected. When she stopped to ask the way, the villagers would silently point out the direction while continuing to stare curiously and unblinkingly.

The Chief was an eccentric. He lived on the outskirts of Obo. His spies told him that strangers were looking for him. The Chief did not like uninvited any guests. In fact, he did not like guests at all. He wondered whether he should cast a spell and kill the strangers before they even reached his home. Such was his power that it would only take a relatively simple spell. The Chief decided that that would be too easy. He would amuse himself and turn them into the first creature that came to mind when he set eyes upon them. It was a punishment he often meted out on those who dared to annoy him. One could never tell if the goat eating silently in the yard, the cock crowing at dawn, or even the frog croaking a song in the pond was some hapless person who had been unlucky enough to feel the Chief's wrath. The Chief mischievously awaited the strangers' arrival.

Meanwhile, Emokpagbe and Emokpolo journeyed on. Emokpolo was relieved that their journey was soon to end. They stopped by a stream. Both mother and son bathed in the cool, refreshing waters. Emokpolo removed from her pouch some black soap her grandmother had given to her. She remembered the old lady's instructions : "Only use this soap a few hours before you meet the Chief of Obo, for its powers will soon wear off." Her grandmother had never told her exactly what the soap was supposed to do and Emokpolo had never asked.

She felt refreshed for the first time in several weeks when she stepped out of the water. Humming contentedly to herself, she dressed. What she did not know was that the magic of the soap had already begun to work. Anyone else would have seen a woman dressed not in rags but in the most radiant and glamorous robes.

The Chief was waiting to see the two ragged, dirty people his spies had told him had entered the village. He was not prepared for the sight that met his eyes. For the first time, his stony, cold heart fluttered as he took in Emokpolo's radiant beauty emphasized by her exquisite garments. Before he

could stop himself, the thought flitted through his mind that she looked like a royal princess.

Emokpolo was not aware of what was going through the Chief's mind. She went up to him and knelt politely in greeting. The Chief stared down at her with his cold, beady eyes. Emokpolo hurriedly reached into her bag and brought out some kolanuts, a traditional gift offering which she humbly offered to the Chief. The Chief took in the nuts, and looked from Emokpolo to Emokpagbe. He realized that he had lost. His honour dictated he would have to let them live. Now he was bored with them.

The Chief received the kolanuts ungraciously and called a messenger, "Escort them back to where they came from. See that no harm comes to them." He stood up to leave.

Emokpolo said urgently, "Please, sir, we have come a long way. I know you can heal my son. The Chief began to walk away. The messenger stepped forward. Emokpolo pushed him away and hurried after the Chief. In a fit of desperation she clung to his sleeve. "Please do not send us away like this," she begged. "Look at my son, have pity on him. He grows weaker daily. If you don't help, no one can and he will die."

The Chief tried to ignore Emokpolo, but she was persistent. Everywhere he went, she followed. Finally, he asked impatiently, "How do you know I could cure your son?"

"Because I know you can...you are the only one that can," Emokpolo replied simply.

Flattery has been known to soften even the hardest of hearts, for people will always want praise. The Chief was no exception - he was impressed at Emokpolo's absolute faith in his powers. Slowly, he began to relent.

"Let me look at the boy," he said gruffly. At the expression of joy on her face, he quickly added, "I'm not promising anything." Emokpolo nodded quickly, but she knew she had won.

And so, Emokpolo left Emokpagbe behind with the Chief. Her work done, she returned home with several escorts and many gifts.

The Chief began to try and cure Emokpagbe, but treatment was slow. Every morning and evening the Chief would pick a variety of herbs and roots from the forest. These he would mix into a liquid and give to the boy to drink. Slowly, strength returned to Emokpagbe's wasting limbs. Soon he was strong enough to accompany the Chief into the forest in the search for herbs. As they searched, the Chief would point out to Emokpagbe the different plants, herbs and roots. He would explain each of their healing properties.

Weeks turned into months, months into years. The relationship between Emokpagbe and the Chief strengthened. The Chief came to look on the young man as the son he had never had. Emokpagbe learned to speak again.

By the time he was healed, the bond between the two had so strengthened that Emokpagbe chose to remain with the Chief, learning the secrets of nature and the mysteries of the supernatural. As time passed, the Chief allowed Emokpagbe to know secrets he had never before shared with a living soul.

Three years went by. Emokpagbe had no desire to return home, but then he received a message from his father. The Enogie urged Emokpagbe to come home. He told his son that he had not many years left to live and there were secrets that needed to be passed on. Emokpagbe knew then that he had been neglecting his duty. As the eldest son of an Enogie, it was his duty to be at his father's side, learning about the title he would one day inherit. Emokpagbe got the Chief's consent and made immediate preparations to return home.

The day arrived for Emokpagbe to leave. He had packed his things. It now only remained for him to say goodbye. Emokpagbe went looking for the Chief. After searching for a while, he finally found his mentor sitting alone in his shrine.

"Baba," Emokpagbe called, standing at the door. The Chief looked up slowly, creasing his face as if the effort hurt. "You are ready?" he asked.

Emokpagbe nodded, stepping into the dark chamber. "I have come to thank you, Baba, for everything."

The Chief took in Emokpagbe's soft youthful features. He wondered if it were true what the Oracle had just told him. But then, how could it not be? Had the Oracle ever lied to him? He had received a warning not to let Emokpagbe leave the village alive, for, if he were to do so, the young man would one day return to kill him.

"Baba," Emokpagbe called, innocent to the workings of the Chief's mind, "is something the matter?"

The Chief heard the voice as if from a great distance. He looked up. The eyes that stared back into his were sincere. The Chief then realized how much Emokpagbe had changed him. Once he would have not thought twice about cutting short Emokpagbe's life. After all, he had killed dozens in his time for far less. But Emokpagbe had touched the Chief in a way that had never before happened to him. He knew then that he could not heed the words of the Oracle. The Chief stood up. He put an arm around Emokpagbe's shoulders and said, "Come, my son, I will walk with you to the road."

Years passed. Emokpagbe re-settled in his town. Eventually his father died and he became the Enogie. For the next few years he ruled the people wisely and well. He was a fine young man, well loved and admired by his subjects.

Meanwhile back in Obo, the Chief came to terms with the absence of his beloved Emokpagbe. He reverted to his solitary lifestyle. As the years went by, he lapsed into his old ways. Quick to lose his temper, he was once more feared throughout the land. Without Emokpagbe's even temper and restraining influence, many hapless souls became the victims of the Chief's wrath. One such victim was a young woman named Adesuwa.

It was a day like any other and the Chief passed by a market as he journeyed from one town to another. He happened to see Adesuwa and became immediately attracted to her. Unknown to him, the Oba of Benin had also fallen in love with this beautiful young woman. Impulsively, the Chief went over to

53

talk to Adesuwa. Adesuwa might have been very beautiful, but she was also very tactless. She saw the middle-aged, unattractive man who stood before her and she decided that she did not wish to talk to him. And in no uncertain terms she told him so. The Chief persisted, but Adesuwa got ruder and ruder. Eventually the Chief became so annoyed that he killed her.

News of Adesuwa's death reached the Oba of Benin. He swore to avenge the death of the woman he loved. In those days, Benin was a strong and powerful empire. Villages for hundreds of miles outside the empire feared and respected the power of Benin. The Oba called his war chiefs and told them that he wanted the Chief of Obo brought before him. Obo was a small unimportant village, so the war chiefs felt that capturing its leader would pose no problems.

An elder at the meeting tried to caution the overconfident chiefs, but failed. "I have heard the Chief has powerful medicine. Our job might not be as simple as it seems," he said.

The others scoffed. "Who is more powerful than the Oba of Benin?" they asked.

And so it was reported back to the Oba that capturing the Chief would be easy.

The Benin war chief ordered his warriors to surround Obo. With a hand-picked group of fine young men, he marched on the village. To their surprise, they encountered no resistance. There were no signs of a defending army. Everything was calm tranquil. The villagers hardly seemed to notice the strangers entering their land.

The general and his men reached the Chief's home. They found him tending his goats.

"In the name of the Oba of Benin, we come to arrest you to face trial for the death of Adesuwa," the general told the Chief as he prepared to give the order for his men to capture the Chief.

To the surprise of the army general, the war chiefs who stood a little distance away, and the warriors who stood behind them, the Chief's only reaction was a derisory laugh.

The general then gave the order and soldiers stepped forward to arrest the Chief. Then a strange thing happened.

The Chief blew a powdery substance in their faces. The men spluttered and coughed, trying to get the dust out of their eyes. Then, to the increasing amazement of all who stood there that afternoon, the soldiers slowly changed into dry, brown leaves which fluttered to the ground. A sudden gust of wind swept them up and blew them away. This can't be happening, the general thought as he ordered more of his men forward. Obediently they ran toward the Chief, only to meet with the same fate.

The general found his well armed army powerless in the face of the Chief's amazing and mysterious powers. Finally, he admitted defeat and withdrew his remaining men.

The Oba listened in annoyance and frustration as he heard how the Chief had defeated his finest soldiers. The Chief's powers had left the war chiefs confused and bewildered. They had no advice left to give the Oba so he resorted to consulting the Oracle. He was told that the only person who could kill the Chief of Obo was a man called Emokpagbe.

"Who is this Emokpagbe?" the Oba asked his advisers. He was informed that Emokpagbe was the Enogie of a village which had been conquered by Benin. The Oba had absolute power over every citizen in his kingdom. He immediately sent for Emokpagbe and ordered him to kill the Chief of Obo.

Emokpagbe knew that to refuse to carry out a direct order from the Oba meant instant death. But the Chief was the last person Emokpagbe wanted to kill. What crime had his old mentor committed? he wondered. He knew the Chief was quick to anger and impetuous in the extreme. Emokpagbe decided that he would go to Obo and have a long talk with the Chief. Perhaps then they could work out what to do next. And so, Emokpagbe went back to Obo.

He arrived to find the Chief's compound deserted. "Baba," he called, as he made his way through the familiar grounds, "Baba, it is me, Emokpagbe." Emokpagbe entered the house and walked through the rooms which had once been his home. Everything seemed to be as he had left it. In fact, it seemed as if he had never left. All the time he called out to the Chief.

No one answered. Emokpagbe entered the courtyard. It too was deserted. He walked further into the yard. Then he stopped, spinning round suddenly at the sound of a footfall. Emokpagbe found himself face to face with the Chief of Obo.

"What do you want, Emokpagbe?" the Chief asked softly, his hand on his sword.

"Baba, they sent me for you."

"So this is how you repay me," the Chief replied, circling around Emokpagbe with a look of utter contempt.

"I only came to talk, Baba."

"Liar!" the Chief spat at Emokpagbe, remembering the words of the Oracle: 'If you let him go, he will one day return to kill you.' "I know why you have come."

"Baba, please listen to me," Emokpagbe pleaded.

"Never! You will have to kill me first," the Chief shouted, mad with rage. In one lightning movement he whipped out his sword. The surface caught the sun and blinded Emokpagbe momentarily.

"Do not let it come to this," Emokpagbe pleaded, stepping back, out of the blinding glare of the sun's reflection. The

Chief held his sword before him and prepared to strike Emokpagbe. In a moment, Emokpagbe had drawn his sword. He parried with it and the blade of the Chief's sword caught the side of it, just missing Emokpagbe's head. The fight had begun.

The two fought under the fierce glare of the blazing sun. It was a vicious fight that went on for several hours. Both were equally matched. Neither could gain the upper hand which each so desperately needed. The day wore on and the fight continued. Feet kicked up the red, dusty earth which formed a haze around the fighters. The smell of the battle rose in the air as blood and sweat mingled.

And then, as dusk approached, the Chief took a fatal step backwards. His sandals caught on a stone. He lost his balance

and fell, landing flat on his back. In a moment, Emokpagbe stood over him, sword raised in the air.

"Kill me and you die: that is the curse of the gods," the Chief cried.

Emokpagbe knew that, if he allowed the Chief to rise, he would kill him in an instant, so he lowered his sword and slashed at the Chief, cutting off his head with a single stroke...

Worn out from the fight, Emokpagbe decided to rest in Obo for a while before setting off for Benin, so he gave the head of the Chief to a messenger. he told him to take it to the Oba of Benin, to show that the task had been successfully carried out. Obediently, the messenger took possession of the macabre object and hurried on to Benin.

Once in Benin, the messenger gained an immediate audience with the Oba. He brought out the head. "Your majesty," he said, "I have done as you ordered."

The Oba looked at the head. He was satisfied that it was indeed that of the Chief. Pleased, he ordered the messenger to be well rewarded.

A few days later, Emokpagbe arrived at Benin. As he made his way through the wide streets to the palace he wondered at the cold welcome he received. There were no crowds, no welcoming party. Alone, he entered the palace. He was made to wait several hours before being granted an audience with the Oba who did not seem particularly interested to see him.

"Your Majesty, I have done as you ordered."

"Who are you?" the Oba asked scornfully.

"Emokpagbe - you ordered me to kill the Chief of Obo," Emokpagbe patiently explained.

"Oh yes," the Oba snorted. "Are you not a man that you should run from the battlefield and allow your subordinates to carry out your tasks?"

Emokpagbe was confused. "What, your Majesty?"

"We were informed of the true story. Your messenger even said that, when you heard that the Chief was dead, you would come before me and try to take the glory. Begone, you lowly coward, before I have you killed," the Oba cried.

Emokpagbe left and returned to his town, bitterly wounded at the way he had been treated in Benin. He immediately banned all the women of his town from using the market at Benin.

The Oba of Benin came to hear of Emokpagbe's ban and was furious. Who, he thought, was Emokpagbe to dare to divide his kingdom? Warriors were sent to capture Emokpagbe and kill him.

And so it happened. Emokpagbe was killed within the year. His body was flung into the Igbaghon river by the Benin soldiers. Time had healed the wounds of Igbaghon, the troubled goddess of the waters whose story is told in "Revenge of the River Goddess". She received the body and made Emokpagbe immortal. Old men say that they live forever below the river.

Eturohun

Along time ago, there lived a prince named Eturohun. He was the son of an Enogie or a Duke who had fallen on hard times, so Eturohun farmed for his living. One fine day, Eturohun made his way to his farm as usual at the break of dawn. As he worked in the field, he heard someone call his name. Eturohun turned towards the sound. The field had been cleared, but he could see no one in it. A stout iroko tree was all that was left in the centre of the field to provide some shade from the fierce midday sun. Eturohun shrugged, sure that his imagination must be playing tricks on him. He continued to hoe the ground.

"Eturohun! Eturohun!" The voice, though a harsh whisper, was loud and clear. Eturohun stood up abruptly. Now he was sure that he was not imagining things. He threw down his hoe and walked towards the iroko tree. There was no one about. Eturohun stood there puzzled. He scratched his head, wondering what was going on. He looked around and listened. All he could hear were the sounds of the wind whispering through the iroko tree, crickets chattering to one another, and birds singing. Eturohun once again picked up his hoe.

Suddenly the voice called out again. "Eturohun!!" This time the whisper was louder and even more commanding. There was no mistaking it. Eturohun threw down his hoe.

"Who is there?" he cried, startled.

"I am over here," the voice hissed. Eturohun followed the sound with his eyes. He saw a little clump of grass at the far corner of the field. As Eturohun walked towards it, he thought surely no one could hide behind that little clump of grass and not be seen.

Eturohun walked around the little clump. His eyes opened wide at the sight before him. Facing him was a decapitated human head. It lay at an angle on the ground, its eyes closed.

Eturohun stooped to get a better look. "What are you? *Who* are you?" he asked, amazed. Not a sound came out of the head which continued to lie there unmoving. Eturohun picked up

a stick and prodded the head. The eyes immediately sprang open.

"Ouch, that hurt!" cried the head, annoyed, "What did you have to do that for?"

"I'm...I'm...well, sorry" replied Eturohun, unsure.

"So you should be ," the head muttered, shifting onto its side. It yawned and promptly closed its eyes.

Eturohun continued to gaze at the head in amazement.

"Who are you? Who did this to you? What are you?" he asked.

"Do you have to ask so many questions?" the head muttered, slightly irritably. It opened its eyes and looked straight at Eturohun. "Phew! it's hot" it complained, "Give me some water."

"Of course," Eturohun replied, removing the flask from his waistband. He opened it and started to pass it over. Then he stopped, realizing that the head had no hands.

"What's the matter now?" the head asked irritably, "Are you giving me the water or not?" Then the head rolled itself over so its face was skyward. It opened its mouth so wide that Eturohun could see right down its throat. Eturohun knelt forward and began to pour the water into the mouth. "Gently now, gently," the head gurgled between mouthfuls. Eturohun wondered where the water went, but he was too polite to ask.

When the head had had enough, it simply closed its mouth. As Eturohun watched, the head rolled itself onto its neck. Eturohun put his flask away. He hoped the drink would have made the head better-tempered. "Are you all right?" he ventured. The head did not reply, but simply burped. Eturohun decided to try again. "How did you know my name? he asked.

"There are lots of things I know. It is never wise to tell all that one knows." The head the rolled onto its side and closed its eyes.

Eturohun watched it for a few moments. Then, realising that it was not going to say any more, he prepared to stand up. The head called after him. "Go in peace, Eturohun," it said, "But you must never tell any one at home what you have seen or heard this day."

Eturohun agreed, gathered up his tools and ran home, thinking only of what he had seen.

The first thing that Eturohun did when he reached the city was to go to the palace. He spoke to the Oba, telling him of the amazing thing he had seen. "Your Majesty," he said, "I saw a wonderful thing today. There was a human head on my farm. It spoke to me, called my name, even drank my water, yet it was only a head with no body."

The Oba and his attendants laughed at Eturohun.

"How dare a drunkard come before the Oba?" some onlookers said. "Could he be mad?" others asked.

Eturohun ignored their snide comments. Appealing to the Oba he said "I am neither drunk nor mad, Your Majesty. To prove what I am telling you is the truth, why don't you send some of your servants with me as witnesses?"

Eturohun's persuasive manner succeeded in swaying the Oba. He decided to give Eturohun the benefit of the doubt, so he agreed to send two of his servants with Eturohun to see the amazing talking human head. Before they departed, the Oba warned Eturohun that if it was a lie, he would pay dearly for it.

Eturohun hurried back to his farm with the Oba's servants. The head lay on its side behind the clump of grass exactly as he had left it. Eturohun smiled victoriously. "*See*, I was not lying." he said.

"Yes, but you said it *spoke* to you," the messengers replied.

"A decapitated human head is not in itself remarkable. Anyone could have put it here. But if it should talk, now that would be a different matter entirely."

"Oh, but it *will* talk," Eturohun replied confidently.

The messengers looked disbelievingly at each other. The head lay there, eyes closed, completely still.

"In the name of His Majesty, the Oba of Benin," the messengers said, "We order you to speak." They stared hard at the head, but there was no movement at all. They tried again. "Speak, we command you, in the name of His Excellency, the Oba." The head remained mute.

Seven times, the messengers commanded the head in the name of the Oba to speak, but not once did a sound come from its mouth.

Eturohun was now desperate. He called to the head, telling it to remember him as the one who had given it water. The head remained mute. Eturohun was now in a panic. "Wait it will talk, it *must*," he appealed to the messengers. He knelt by the head and begged it to speak, to utter just one word, one little word. But the head lay there, completely immobile. Not a word came forth from its tightly pursed lips.

Finally, the messengers had had enough. They returned to the palace and went straight to the Oba. They told him that there was no talking head on Eturohun's farm. The Oba was annoyed that Eturohun should try to make a fool of him. He condemned Eturohun to death.

As he was being led out to the place of his execution, Eturohun cried out in anguish, "You can't do this to me. I am the son of an Enogie. It is against our laws!"

The executioner paused. He reported what he had heard to a prison officer who reported it to the Oba.

Now in Benin law and custom it was against the law to

execute the child of a nobleman. The Oba ordered a hasty investigation to find out if it was true, that Eturohun was really who he claimed to be. It was proved that Eturohun spoke the truth - he was indeed the son of an Enogie.

The Oba had no choice but to order Eturohun to be set free. Before Eturohun left for home, the Oba warned him that it was only his royal blood which saved his life. He told Eturohun to go in peace, but to be careful to tell no further lies. After thanking the Oba, Eturohun left for home, a much wiser man.

There is a common saying among the Binis:

"It is not wise to tell all that one sees, nor is it wise to say all that one thinks."

The Beautiful Princess

A long, long time ago, there lived a powerful Oba. He had many wives, many servants and great wealth. But the King was not a happy man. Every day he became more and more miserable because he did not have the one thing he most desired - a child. In all the years he had been married, not one of his many wives had been able to give birth to a baby.

One day, the Oba sent for the Oracle. He offered sacrifices to appease his ancestors and asked the old medicine man to speak to the gods to find out why he had not been blessed with a child. The medicine man brought out his divining palm kernels. He said some prayers and threw the kernels on the ground. Then he read the message that was revealed to him.

The medicine man went into the forest and searched for herbs and wild roots. He ground these into a paste and added some native chalk. He took it to the Oba. "Your Majesty," he said respectfully, "this is the medicine the gods have told me to give to you. Put it in a big basin and add some alligator pepper. Then call all your wives and tell each to scoop out and eat a handful. Be sure to treat all your wives equally," he cautioned the Oba as he hobbled out of the palace.

The Oba thanked the medicine man and had the paste emptied into a large bowl and mixed with alligator pepper. Then he sent for his wives.

The wives came, a babbling, squabbling mass. Each was eager to take a share of the medicine. They gathered round the bowl and ate up its contents greedily, not heeding the Oba's words that they should take only a handful. They thought that the more they ate, the better their chances of getting pregnant, so they pushed and shoved and fought to gobble down as much as they could. Soon it was all gone.

Now the Oba had one other wife whom he had completely forgotten. Her name was Idris. She was the least favorite of his wives. She was bullied and abused by the other women in the harem who were a particularly unpleasant bunch. The Oba had never showered her with gifts as he did his other wives, so she wore old, faded clothes which people said did not become a royal wife.

No one bothered to let her know that the wives had been summoned. Nobody thought it important enough. It was by

chance that Idris saw the procession of excited, chattering women. She stopped a messenger who told her about the message from the Oba. Idris decided to follow the other wives, but she kept a discreet distance.

Idris hid behind a window and watched the women gobble up the medicine. She was afraid to come out because she knew she would be bullied and beaten if she did. When the wives had taken their fill of the medicine, they left the room., wiping their lips and talking excitedly. Each boasted how much she had eaten. Idris waited till the room was empty, before creeping out of her hiding-place and up to the basin. When she looked down, the bowl was empty. Sadly she knelt by it and scraped the little that was left from the bottom. She licked her fingers, but barely tasted the medicine as there was so little left.

The messengers went to the Oba and told him that his orders had been carried out. He waited hopefully for news about the condition of his wives. After a few weeks he received a message that all the women were pregnant, including Idris. The Oba was overjoyed. He offered sacrifices to thank his ancestors. At last, his prayers had been answered.

The Oba waited happily for his wives to give birth. He was eager to hold a bouncing baby boy or girl in his arms. The months passed, and his joy knew no bounds. He showered his wives with gifts of coral beads and fine cloth. All except for Idris, whom he completely forgot about. She withdrew to her private chambers, away from the spiteful, bullying women who had made her life a complete misery.

One by one, the Oba's wives went into labour. There was great excitement in the palace. The Oba paced about his private chambers as he waited impatiently for the messenger to bring him news of the birth of his children. The hours passed, but no one came. The Oba would not eat, so eager was he to hear the news. At sunrise, he was still awake, waiting for a messenger who never arrived. Finally in annoyance he sent one of his sword-bearers to go to the harem and find out why he had no news about the birth of his children.

The sword-bearer was gone for less than a hour. He came back with a grave expression on his face. "What did you find out?" the Oba demanded.

"Your Majesty," the sword-bearer bowed respectfully before him, "I have bad news...terrible news." He shook his head sadly. The Oba leaned forward. The sword-bearer continued, "When I got to the gates of the harem, there was no rejoicing. Instead, I found an alarming gloom and sadness." The Oba listened in horror as the sword-bearer went on.

The Oba's wives had indeed given birth. But their punishment for their greed was the monsters they were cursed to bear. Creatures so vile and horrible that one midwife had dropped dead from shock. A cold hand clutched at the Oba's heart as the sword-bearer ended his story. Am I never to father a child? the Oba thought sadly as he ordered a period of mourning.

But unknown to the Oba, not all his wives had given birth. Idris was still pregnant. Though she kept to herself, she was aware of what had happened to the other wives. It scared her that the same thing might happen to her.

One day, Idris needed some wood to light a fire. As she had no personal maids, she took her machete and went to the forest. As she was hacking at a tree, she felt a sharp pain rush through her stomach. She dropped the machete and cried out in agony. Clutching her stomach, she sank to the ground.

A palmwine tapper happened to be high up in a palm tree collecting the juice from the tree into his gourd. When he heard the scream, he immediately came down to investigate the noise and found Idris. She was in labour. The pain tore at her stomach - she was twisting and contorting in agony. The palmwine tapper was a gentle, kind man. He saw immediately that Idris was about to give birth, so he gathered some dried leaves to make a bed for her to lie on. Idris was screaming and shouting in terror. The palmwine tapper mistakenly thought it was because of the pain of childbirth. He could not understand why she kept gasping, "Please, God, don't curse *me* too."

And so, with the palmwine tapper's help, Idris gave birth. She could not believe it when she saw her perfectly formed, beautiful baby girl. The palmwine tapper took the baby to a nearby stream and bathed it, and then Idris wrapped it in some of her faded clothes. She held the baby and gazed down tenderly at it, taking in its delicate features. She named the child Adesuwa. She was so thankful that she had been blessed with a perfect baby girl.

It was getting late, so the palmwine tapper offered to help the new mother home, but a sudden realization hit Idris. What would happen if she took her child to the palace? Surely those jealous, spiteful women would try to destroy the child. Idris was well aware how much they hated her already. She dreaded to think of what would happen when they found out that she had done what none of them had been able to do - given the Oba a child. With a sudden cry of anguish, she clutched the innocent, sleeping infant to her breast. Then she looked up into the warm, kind face of the palmwine tapper. Idris could hold back her fears no longer. She told him everything about her life in the palace. The palmwine tapper listened in silence and by the time she had finished he had begun to understand some of her fears.

"I'll help you in whatever way I can," he said.

"Then take my child," Idris urged impulsively, thrusting

the child into his arms, "Take her and bring her up as yours. Do not let her return to the palace till she is grown."

The palmwine tapper was startled. "But..." he began, "I do not know anything about children...I..."

"Give her love, that's all she needs," Idris said stroking the child's cheek fondly. She bent to plant kisses on the warm face. "Goodbye, my darling," she whispered as she got to her feet.

And so the palmwine tapper took the baby to his home and brought her up as his own. Idris went back to the palace, but she never told anyone about her child. Everyone assumed that she had given birth to a monster and was so ashamed of the fact that she must have buried it out in the forest.

Years passed and Adesuwa grew up. News reached the Oba that there was an extremely beautiful girl living in his kingdom. He was curious and decided that he had to see this girl whose beauty was being talked about in the four corners of his kingdom.

Adesuwa was brought before the Oba. He was immediately struck by her perfect beauty, her smooth, dark skin, her youth and innocence. As the Oba gazed at her, he wondered why a lowly palmwine tapper could be blessed with such a perfect child. How thoroughly unfair life was, he thought miserably.

When Adesuwa left the Oba's presence, he continued to see her in his mind's eye. He lost all interest in matters of state. All he could think of was Adesuwa. Finally he reached a decision. He would take Adesuwa's hand in marriage. With such a vision of perfect youth and beauty, she was sure to give him the child he longed for so desperately.

The Oba ordered Adesuwa to be brought before him. Adesuwa knelt respectfully and told him that she could not marry him.

The Oba was amazed. Such impertinence, he thought. "And why not?" he asked. Adesuwa replied humbly, "Because I am your daughter, sire." This revelation astounded not only the Oba, but all the attendants and courtiers who were present. There was an immediate buzz as everyone started to speak at once. News of the girl's assertion spread through the palace like wildfire. Soon everyone was talking about it.

The Oba did not believe Adesuwa, but he did not know what to do. He paced about his chambers all night thinking. Finally, at dawn the next day, he consulted the Oracle. Adesuwa's claim was confirmed. This made the Oba even more confused because all his wives rushed to him to claim that Adesuwa was her child. So the Oba asked the Oracle to reveal Adesuwa's mother. The Oracle told the Oba to order each of his wives to cook a dish. These were to be arranged on a table outside the harem. Adesuwa was to be brought out and told to choose a dish. The one she chose would most definitely have been cooked by her real mother.

All the wives eagerly scurried away to begin preparing the most elaborate meals they could, buying the choicest cuts of meat, the best vegetables, spices and herbs. All day they cooked, discarding dishes if they did not taste just right. The competition in the royal kitchens was fierce.

Idris also cooked, but she did not have any money to spend in the market, so she contented herself with using the scraps that the other wives discarded.

Evening came, and the women dished up their offerings. A table was set, covered with the finest, whitest cloth. The other wives lined up their dishes on the table. Then Idris brought out hers. She could not afford fine bronze dishes. So her meal was served in a pot of baked clay. The other wives laughed at her meager offering. There was no room left on the table, so Idris put her bowl on the ground by one end of the table.

Adesuwa was brought out and told to choose a dish. She stood before the table with her hands behind her back, her head held up high, a picture of serenity and dignity. Slowly she began to walk down the length of the table, taking in all the exotic and elaborate dishes. The wives watched with bated breath. Sometimes Adesuwa would hesitate for more than a moment at a dish. Then, just as the people watching began to think that she was going to taste it, she would shake her head and move on. Each wife gave a sign of disappointment as Adesuwa dismissed her dish.

Finally, Adesuwa reached the end of the table. Nothing had so far tickled her appetite. She was about to walk away when she saw the earthenware bowl placed on the ground. Adesuwa only had to look at it once for a smile to light up her face. She sat down on the floor and began to eat, licking her lips as she enjoyed the meal. The other wives watched in shock as Adesuwa happily finished the meager contents of the bowl.

It was now agreed by everyone that Adesuwa's mother was Idris. The Oba was happy that his one wish was fulfilled - he had the child he had always longed for. But he was also ashamed at the way he had treated Idris. He swore to her that he would make up for his cruel behaviour. To prove that he meant what he said, he banished all the jealous wives to remote areas of his kingdom where they could cause no more trouble. The Oba was now free to live happily with Idris and their daughter Adesuwa.

The Wicked Servant Girl

There was once a young woman called Eniye who had been betrothed to a man in a neighbouring village. When the time came for Eniye to go to her fiance's house, she was accompanied by her younger sister, Idia, and a servant girl.

Now Eniye and Idia were the best of friends. They talked and laughed on the long walk. Eniye promised Idia many things in their new home, a house of her own, servants to look after her, plenty of beautiful cloth and coral beads. Eniye could well afford all this because her fiance was a wealthy man. The servant girl walked a few feet behind the two young women, listening enviously to everything that was said.

The sun began to set as the three women neared their destination. As they passed by a large river, the servant girl called her mistress. "Madam," she said, with downcast eyes hiding her insincerity.

"Yes, what is it?" Eniye asked gently.

"I hope you won't think me rude, Madam, but I thought that nothing should spoil your husband's first impression of you." Eniye listened as the servant girl continued, "Madam, you are so beautiful. The sun shines out of your eyes. Your skin is as smooth and soft as a newborn baby's...but, Madam, there is one thing which is not quite right. We have walked all day and your feet have gathered dust." Eniye looked down at her feet.

The servant girl pointed to the river. "Surely the gods must be in agreement, for them to have placed a stream at such a convenient spot."

Eniye thanked the servant girl for being so thoughtful. She went over to the banks of the river and bent down to begin washing her feet. Idia sat on the trunk of a tree, singing softly as she daydreamed about her new life. The servant girl crept up behind Eniye and, before anyone knew what was happening, had pushed her mistress into the river.

Idia was awoken from her daydream by a scream. She rushed to the banks of the river, yelling for her sister whom she saw disappearing below the surface of the water. Tears streaming down her face, she turned to the servant girl. A frightening sight met her eyes. The servant girl had always been well built, but, as she towered over Idia, she seemed positively monstrous. She looked down at Idia with a face that was hard and cold. Her narrow, little eyes seemed to pierce through Idia's soul. they shone with evil. The servant girl roughly pulled Idia away from the banks of the river.

"If you ever tell anyone what has happened here today, I promise I will kill you with my bare hands," she threatened through clenched teeth.

Idia whimpered as the servant girl pushed her roughly onto the path. "Come on, let's go," she snarled. As Idia stumbled, the servant girl told her, "I am now Eniye."

"No!" Idia shook her head as the realization of what the servant girl now planned to do hit her. Idia did not see it coming, but the slap that landed on her face was enough to send her flying. As she lay in the dirt, the servant girl came up to her and kicked her hard in the ribs. Idia screamed, then she was pulled up roughly. The servant girl's face was barely two inches away. Idia shivered at the evil glint in her eyes.

"I am now Eniye ." the servant girl repeated.

"But people will know," stammered Idia.

"How? You keep your big mouth shut and no one will ever be any the wiser. Come on, don't be so lazy - pick up my things."

And so Idia and the servant girl walked the last few metres and entered the village.

There was a welcoming party waiting for the new arrivals. The servant girl introduced herself as Eniye and was warmly greeted by everyone in her new family including her husband-to-be Nosa. He was a little uneasy as he embraced her, but he kept his reservations to himself. He had been told that his new wife was very beautiful, but this girl was not. She had a hard, masculine face with a crooked nose. There were two extremely unattractive moles on her chin, out of which grew a few scraggly hairs. She smiled lovingly at Nosa, but he noticed that the smile did not reach her narrow, ratlike, little eyes.

The marriage celebrations had begun. Nosa was the son of a wealthy and popular man in the village, so everyone joined in. Nosa decided that he would not spoil the people's fun by criticizing his new wife, so he shrugged off his reservations and joined in the revelries.

But things did not improve. In fact, they became steadily worse. Nosa and the servant girl set up home together and soon Nosa realized that his new wife was lazy. She liked to do nothing but lie out in the sun all day. It was her servant, Idia, who was made to do all the work. Nosa's wife could not even be bothered to prepare her husband's meals. Idia prepared the meals, Idia cleaned, Idia did everything, yet all day long

Nosa's wife would yell and scream at her. That would be bad enough if that were all, but it was not, not at all. Nosa's wife was crude and badly behaved. Every time Nosa took her out, she embarrassed him by fighting with his friends and their wives. So gradually people started to stay away and the invitations got fewer and fewer until they dried up completely. It reached a stage where Nosa even began to dislike coming home. It seemed his wife could quarrel about anything, no matter how trivial, and she would go on and on... Nosa had not yet admitted it to himself, but he was miserable.

One morning, before the first cock-crow, Idia went off to the river to fetch some water for her day's tasks. She set down her pot by the bank of the river and started to weep as she remembered what had happened to her poor sister. She then began to sing softly, calling for her sister, asking why she had left her alone in this troubled, unfair world.

The song was so sad that the birds on the treetops wept. A strange silence descended on the forest as the animals stopped playing to listen to the clear, sad voice that sang of such unhappiness. Even the wind seemed to be holding its breath.

Then, all of a sudden there was a rippling in the river. The waters seemed to part and up rose Eniye. She swam gracefully to the banks. "Idia, why are you so sad?" she asked.

Idia stopped singing, startled. "Eniye! Eniye!" she called.

"Shhhh, not so loud," Eniye said, "You called and I came. What is troubling you, sister dear?"

And so Idia began to narrate her troubles. She told how the servant girl had taken Eniye's place and everything that had happened since. Eniye listened, sad that her younger sister had been so ill-treated.

The two young women talked for a while. Then Eniye took Idia's water pot and disappeared down below. A few minutes

later, she rose again to the surface of the water. The pot was filled with clear, sparkling water. And down at the bottom were the brightest, most radiant coral beads.

Idia whistled on her way back to the village. For the first time since she had arrived at the village she felt happy. She did her chores without complaining. The servant girl watched Idia. She was puzzled at the young woman's changed behaviour. She increased Idia's chores, thinking spitefully, "That should wipe the smile off her face." To her increasing annoyance, it did not.

The next morning, Idia woke up even earlier to go to the stream. She knelt by the bank of the river and began to sing. Once again, her sister came up from the river bed. The two laughed and talked just like the old times. When it was time for Idia to leave, Eniye took the water pot to the bottom of the river, filled it with fresh, sparkling water and a layer of coral beads.

The same thing happened the next day, and the next. Then, on the sixth day, Eniye told Idia not to come again. For on the seventh day, Eniye would be made immortal, and become a servant goddess of the river forever. It was forbidden for the immortal spirits of the waters to have any contact with humans. Eniye sadly told her sister that she would never be able to see her again.

Idia received her pot of water and went back to the village. Her heart was heavy as she thought about what Eniye had told her, but she was determined to find a way to help her sister. Idia realized that the first thing she needed to do was to get someone in the village to believe her story. "But how?" she wondered.

It was a hot afternoon. The sun shone with its customary unblinking gaze. The servant girl lay on a hammock underneath a huge iroko tree. Idia was pounding some millet in the yard. She stared deep into the bowl as her pounding stick broke the grains into thousands of tiny pieces. She was preoccupied. All day she wondered how to get the villagers to believe her story. From the corner of her eye she saw the menfolk make their way to the Chief's compound. Suddenly, she knew what she must do.

Idia looked towards the servant girl who was now snoring gently. She rested the pounding stick against a wall and hurried to the Chief's compound.

There was a hum of conversation from the men in the compound. A boy was distributing calabashes filled with palm wine. Idia saw Nosa was sitting next to the Chief. She ran up to him and began to blurt out her story. All eyes at once turned to Idia. People were amazed that she had the audacity to come before the assembly in this way. "Shut up!" some said. "Throw her out!" others exclaimed. "How dare she?...such rudeness!"

Two of the men in the assembly moved to grab hold of Idia. But Nosa saw something in her face which made him raise up a hand to calm the crowd. "Let her speak," he said.

There was some grumbling. Then the crowd was silent. Idia turned once again to Nosa. "The woman you married is not Eniye!" she exclaimed. She then went on tell Nosa what had happened to the real Eniye.

When she had finished, there was silence. Not surprisingly, no one believed her. Idia saw it in the faces, in the eyes that stared at her. She felt it in the embarrassed silence which hung in the room. "Come to the river tomorrow morning - this one thing is all I ask," she pleaded desperately.

Nosa thought about it for a moment. He took another look at the young girl who knelt before him. Then he realized that, if what she said was true, it made perfect sense, for how else could he explain his wife's behaviour? She did not have the refinement of the daughter of a nobleman. In fact, she was so common it had puzzled him. Nosa knew that he could not have carried on with the charade of his marriage for much longer. He felt relief that Idia had had the courage to bring it out into the open. So he stood up and helped Idia up. "All right," he said. "I will give you the benefit of the doubt. We will come to the river tomorrow."

Idia had got what she wanted. She left the Chief's compound and hurried back to her chores. She found the servant girl still sleeping in the hammock. Satisfied, Idia picked up her stick and continued to pound the millet.

Early the next morning, Idia rushed to the stream. She sat on the banks of the river and waited for her audience. They came soon afterwards, a small procession of men lead by Nosa. They hid behind the reeds and waited.

Idia knelt on the banks of the river. She began to sing. Her soft, melodious voice filled the air. A short while later, she called out "Eniye! Eniye! it is I." She looked at the surface of the river for the familiar ripple. The men peered out from their hiding-places, but nothing happened. The river still continued its unhurried flow downstream.

Idia called louder. "Eniye! Eniye! Why do you not answer?" She looked out over the river, but still there was no ripple. "Am I too late? Who will believe me now?" she wondered sadly. With a heavy heart, she tried one last time. "Eniye! Eniye, please show your face."

Suddenly, the ripples started. Idia held her breath as the waters parted. The men hiding in the bushes could not believe what their eyes told them was true. They saw a beautiful young woman rise out of the water.

Eniye looked at Idia, a frown creasing her brow. "Why have you called me, Idia? Did you forget what I told you yesterday?"

"But I missed you dreadfully, Eniye. I promise, if you talk to me this one time, I won't disturb you again."

Eniye gazed at her younger sister - she looked tired and fragile. The frown lifted from Eniye's face. She swam up to the bank and caressed Idia's face. The two talked for a while, and then Eniye prepared to go back to the goddess of the river.

Idia was suddenly tearful. "What will happen to me when you go? I'll miss you terribly," she cried.

"And I'll miss you too, dear sister, but don't you see that I must go. The water goddess has taken me as her own. There's nothing I can do."

Idia wiped away her tears. She begged Eniye to escort her a short way up the path. Eniye hesitated. She did not want to leave the water. Idia saw Eniye's hesitation. She immediately began to sob.

This softened Eniye's heart. She said "I'll only come a short way. I do not walk too well." She then held out a hand. As Idia helped pull Eniye up onto the river bank, she gasped when she saw that, from the waist down, Eniye now had a huge, impressive fish's tail. Eniye could not walk - she managed to drag herself a little way up the path, but the ground was so slippery that she fell. In that instant, Nosa gave the signal. All the men rushed out of the bushes and, before Eniye knew what was happening, she was caught in a large fishing net.

Eniye was taken back to the village. And after sacrifices were made to appease the goddess of the river, she was eventually allowed to return to the world of mortals. For several days, Eniye was in excruciating pain as her skin moulted. First, the scales that covered her body peeled off. Then her tail dried up and withered away. Finally, the dead skin which once formed Eniye's tail was stripped off to uncover her legs which were now very stiff and sore. Herbal lotions were massaged into the legs and eventually they healed so that Eniye was able to walk on them.

The frightened servant girl was brought to the village

square and made to sit before an open fire. Palm kernels were thrown into the fire. As punishment the servant girl was made to pick the nuts out of the fire with her bare hands. She reached into the fire with her right hand - it was burned. She reached in with her left hand. It also was burned. Then she reached in with her left foot. As it began to burn, she gave a loud, horrifying scream and, before the watching crowd, turned into a very ugly bush dog. She sniffed at her audience before darting into the forest, never to be seen again.

Nosa married the real Eniye and the two sisters remained the best of friends for the rest of their lives.

The Disobedient Child

There once lived a man and a woman. Though they had been married for several years they had no children. Daily the couple prayed to God to grant their dearest wish and bless them with a child. But the years passed and the woman remained barren.

People in the village scoffed at the couple. They advised the man to take another wife who would bear him children. But the man had no interest in what others had to say. He remained devoted to his wife, and together they continued to plead with God to grant them a child.

One day, their prayers were answered. The woman became pregnant and gave birth to a beautiful baby girl. The couple were overjoyed. They adored the child and named her Esareren.

During the naming ceremony, an old seer read Esareren's future in the stones. She told the parents that bad luck would befall the girl on the day before her twelfth birthday. When the anxious couple asked what they must do to protect their child, the seer told them to keep her in the house for the entire day. Not to let her leave the house, even to go down to the stream to fetch water. If this was done, the evil would pass and the child would grow up normally. The parents thanked the old woman and took their daughter home.

As the years passed, Esareren grew even more beautiful. She had lots of hair, a slim, oval face with large, dark eyes. Her teeth seemed perfectly chiselled and were the purest white. She had dimples in her cheeks which made her laugh even more enchanting. No one could fail to be moved by the perfect grace and beauty of Esareren.

Everybody in the village knew Esareren. Everyone spoke of her stunning beauty. Every parent wanted Esareren to be his or her child's best friend. Esareren was welcome at every home, a pleasant guest at every meal. Sometimes parents would gaze at Esareren, drinking in her beauty and then criticize their own children for the littlest wrongdoing. "Why can't you be as well behaved as Esareren?" they would ask, but what they secretly meant was, "Why can't you be as beautiful as Esareren?"

One night, Esareren's mother had a particularly vivid dream. She saw Esareren devoured by the trees in the forest. The woman woke up in a cold sweat. At first she could not understand what the dream meant. Then she realized what day it was. Esareren would be twelve in two days time.

The next morning, the parents prepared to go to the farm as usual. They did not want to alarm Esareren by telling her about the evil that lurked outside, so the mother devised a way to get the child to stay indoors for the whole day. She gave her daughter a huge pile of palm nuts to crack. "And when you've finished that," she continued, "I want you to put this into a pot of boiling hot water. Use the largest pot we have because it will take several hours to cook. You'll know it's cooked because it will be soft," she added, handing Esareren a stone.

"Now promise me," the mother said, gazing into her daughter's lovely eyes, "promise me you will not leave the house till you've completed the tasks I've set you."

"I promise, Mama," Esareren replied.

And so the parents left for the farm. Esareren locked the front door after them. She brought out the huge pile of palm kernels and began shelling them. Esareren was totally absorbed in her task when suddenly she was interrupted by a persistent knocking at the window. "Who is there?" she asked, coming to stand by the wooden shutters.

"Us," a gaggle of girlish voices chorused, "Come out and play, Esareren."

"I can't," Esareren replied, opening one of the wooden shutters to look out at her friends.

"Oh, come on, don't be such a spoil-sport," they urged.

"No, really, I can't. You see my mother has left me with a lot of work to do. She made me promise not to go out and play till I finished it."

"Many hands make light work. Let us in and we'll help."

"Well...all right..." Esareren thought for a moment. She could not see how her mother could object if the girls helped her finish the work. So she opened the door and let the six giggling girls in.

And so, with the help of the girls, all the nuts were soon cracked and washed.

"Now let's go out and play, Esareren," the girls urged, "We've discovered this new place in the woods. You must see it."

But Esareren was still reluctant to leave the house.

"What's the matter now?" We've cracked all the nuts."

"Yes I know you have. But there is one other thing Mama told me to do today." And Esareren took her friends to the back of the house and showed them the stone bubbling in the large metal pot which stood over a coal fire. "She wants me to cook this stone till it's soft," she explained.

"But that's impossible!" exclaimed one girl.

"You can't cook a stone - everyone knows that!" said another indignantly.

"So what am I to do? Until it's cooked, I can't go out and play," Esareren said miserably.

"I have an idea," said one girl. She plucked some cocoa yam leaves and wrapped them around the stone. "This will help the stone to cook. I know that for certain because my grandmother told me. Now you can come out and play."

"Shouldn't we first wait till the stone cooks?" Esareren asked uncertainly.

"Why! It's as good as cooked," the girl replied.

Esareren so wanted to go out and play that she allowed herself to believe that the cocoa yam leaves would cook the stone. She snatched her wrapper and was out of the house in a second.

Esareren and her giggling companions half-ran, half-walked to a nearby stream which was on the edge of a large, dense forest. The girls splashed about and played in the water for a while. Esareren was having such a good time that she completely forgot that she had disobeyed her mother. She was also unaware of something more dangerous. The fact was that the girls who seemed so eager to be with her, the very ones who smiled and joked with her, were hardly friends. They were, in fact, bitterly jealous rivals who plotted to destroy Esareren.

There was a very tall tree which stood by the edge of the stream. After they had dried themselves, the girls started on another game. They dared each other to climb the tree and bring down a particular kind of leaf which only grew at the very top of the tree. Esareren was not too keen on heights, so she decided she would not take her turn. But then she noticed six pairs of eyes staring at her. All the girls urged her to go first. The more Esareren protested, the more insistent they became, practically carrying her to the base of the tree. Finally she decided to climb the tree to get it over and done with.

Slowly, Esareren hoisted herself higher and higher up the tree until she was hidden from the ground by its intertwined leaves and branches. Still she went higher and higher. I can do it, she thought to herself proudly, as she gained confidence, I can win this dare. She was now determined to reach the top and pluck the leaf. And so she climbed higher and higher up the tree.

It was a fascinating world she found up there. Now she did not only hear the birds singing, she could look into the nests in which they perched. The dense branches, heavy with leaves, interlocked with the branches of other trees, forming a canopy. Esareren was entranced. Wait till I tell the girls, she thought as she looked up. The tree stretched even higher. It was taller than any other tree in the forest. Esareren still had some way to go before she reached the top.

Meanwhile, down below, the girls were busy carrying out the next part of their evil plan. They gathered dried pieces of wood and leaves and placed them around the base of the tree. Then they poured some kerosine onto the pile and set fire to it.

The ensuing blaze began to engulf the tree. At first Esareren sniffed at the smell of burning. Then she looked down and saw the raging fire climbing higher and higher, consuming everything in its path. Letting out an almighty scream, she lost her footing and fell right into the fire.

And that was how Esareren was burned to ashes...

A few hours later, Esareren's parents were returning home from the farm. They passed the path which ran along the stream. At the edge of the forest they came upon the tree, once tall and majestic with a hundred leaf-filled branches, but now gutted and dead. Merely a gnarled, hollow shell.

"What could have happened here?" the mother wondered.

Suddenly she was drawn to the foot of the tree, for there lay the most spectacularly white ash she had ever seen. As she reached out a hand to touch it, a voice seemed to sing, in a soft, harsh whisper:

Mother, do not touch
Mother, do not touch
I am the one called Esareren.
I am she who meant so much,
For does not Esareren mean
A child is greater than wealth or glory?

The mother stepped back, she turned to her husband, but he had not heard the voice. The mother was still drawn to the ash. It seemed to have a strange, hypnotic quality. She gazed at its perfect whiteness and, before she knew what was happening, she had stretched out a hand to touch it.

Again, the voice started to sing its sad, harsh whisper. Again, the woman snatched her hand away as if she had touched a bed of burning coals.

Her husband was beginning to get impatient. "Let us hurry home," he urged, "It will be dark soon and Esareren is all alone at home."

But the mother knew that something was not right. As she reluctantly turned to follow her husband, she heard a voice which she recognised as that of the old seer urging her to touch the ashes.

"There is a leaf to your right, a single leaf growing out of the ground. On it is a single drop of blood. When you take the ashes, take also this leaf. At home put both in your daughter's cooking pot."

The mother scooped up the ashes which had a soft, cool feel. She put them into her calabash. She then picked the single leaf which had a single drop of blood on it and, covering the ashes with the leaf, she turned to follow her husband.

At home, Esareren was nowhere to be seen. Panic-stricken, her father rushed all around the house, into the backyard, into the bedrooms, into the living-room, back again into the backyard, all the time calling "Esareren! Esareren!"

The mother went into the backyard where she found the stone still boiling in the pot. She removed the cocoa yam leaves, then poured the ash into the pot, placed the single bloodstained leaf over it and covered the pot. By this time, the husband had left the house and was rushing around to the neighbours, screaming for his beloved daughter. The mother sat patiently by the pot, trusting her instincts. After some time, the same voice told her to open the pot. "And whatever you find in there, take it with thanks," it said.

The mother lifted the lid slightly off the pot. She saw a tiny figure of Esareren sitting on the stone. Esareren looked up at her mother and began to sing in a tiny, tiny voice:

It is me, Esareren.
It is me, Esareren.
I was killed by an enemy.
I was killed because of beauty.

Esareren then looked down sadly, hiding her shame at

being disobedient. the mother gazed at her daughter, so small and fragile. A lump came to her throat.

"Come out, Esareren," she said gently.

Esareren looked up, unsure. She shook her head. "I deserved what I got." She folded her hands in her lap and softly began to hum her song again.

The mother patiently continued to gaze down at her daughter. "Come out, Esareren," she said more definitely.

Esareren stopped singing for a moment. She looked as if deep in thought, then once more she shook her head. "I have annoyed the spirits. I cannot be with you any more."

The mother stood up to her full height. When she looked down at Esareren, her daughter was so tiny she could barely see her.

"Come out! NOW!" she commanded.

Esareren flinched. She looked up at her mother, then rose slowly. She climbed up onto the stone on which she had sat, and reached for the rim of the pot. The mother bent to help her daughter, but Esareren shrugged her away, "No, I must do this myself," she gasped as she struggled to reach the rim of the pot. Several times she lost her footing and fell back into the pot, but she would always get up again, a look of determination on her face. Finally, Esareren managed to grab hold of the rim with one hand. She struggled to pull herself up. Then she was holding onto the rim with two hands. She hoisted herself up, sweating with the effort, and finally managed to bring her body up so she was sitting on the rim. She took a rest for a few moments and looked down at the ground beneath. It looked a thousand miles away.

The mother commanded, "Jump, Esareren!"

Esareren looked down at the drop. It was frightening. She took a moment to steady her nerves and then she jumped. For a while, she felt as if she were flying through the air. Then the most amazing thing happened. Esareren began to grow, taller and taller, until she reached her normal height. Then she landed gently on the ground.

Her mother wept for joy, "Esareren, Esareren," she cried, hugging her daughter as if she would never let her go.

The father heard the noise. He ran back into the house and found his daughter waiting to greet him. All three rejoiced that they were together once more as a family.

And Esareren had learned her lesson. Never again would she disobey her parents.

Legends

In researching these stories, I spoke to an old oral historian whom I call Baba. I do not know exactly how old Baba is, but he could remember being a child during the British punitive expedition in 1897. This would make him over a hundred years old. His memory was incredible and he could name every Oba that had ruled in Benin since the first Oba, Eweka the First, came to power in the twelfth century.

In many old civilizations around the world where the people had no writing of which Benin was no exception, people from the royal courts were selected to learn by heart significant events that were important to the group. These facts were then passed down, generation after generation for hundreds of years. In Benin, this system of recording the history in the minds of chosen people was complimented by the rich body of art, bronzes, ivories and wood which also recorded historical events and important people.

The system of oral tradition had its disadvantages, for, in the retelling, many facts were left out, changed or forgotten. Also the Binis were always very inventive storytellers and, as they wove their tales, fact often merged with fiction to produce the Legends retold in this book.

The Last Ogiso

The Benin Empire was said to have been founded in about 900 AD when a band of travellers left Egypt to find a more secure shelter elsewhere.

On the way, they stopped at many places such as the Sudan, and Ile-Ife. But eventually, they settled in a place which later came to be called Benin.

The rulers were known as the Ogiso, or the Sky rulers. This was because some people actually believed that their rulers were special people who were sent down from the skies to reign.

Very little is known about this period of Benin history. As a result, many myths and legends have developed about the rulers.

The era of the Ogiso, known also as the first period of Benin history, ended in the 1100's when Ogiso Owodo was banished by his people. This is his story...

There was once a ruler in Benin called Ogiso Owodo. He was generally recognized as a weak, ineffective leader. Though he had several wives, he had only one child, a son called Ekaladeran.

The barren wives got increasingly unhappy at this state of affairs. They urged Owodo to send people to the Oracle to find out the cause of their childlessness. Owodo eventually gave in to the pressure and decided to send two chiefs. Esago, Owodo's favourite wife, talked her husband into letting her accompany the chiefs.

Early one cold, windy morning, the three set off on the long trek to seek an audience with the Oracle. The fierce midday sun was baking the earth when they arrived at the isolated clearing in the woods that was the home of the Oracle. They found the wizened old woman who was the voice of the Oracle sitting alone in her shrine. "Welcome, my children," she said in her rusty old voice. She had been expecting them.

Spread out before her were sixteen palm kernels. She indicated that the three should sit before her. Then, scooping up the kernels with one hand, she threw them on the ground so that they formed a random pattern. The three watched, as the old woman stared silently at the nuts, slowly reading the message they revealed to her. Then she frowned - something was not right. She looked up at the three people sitting before her and then quickly down again at the nuts. "That can't be," she muttered to herself. Gathering up the nuts quickly, she threw them once more. Again they formed the same pattern.

"What is it?" one of the chiefs asked.

"Shusuuuuu!" the old woman replied as she scooped the nuts up again. She shook them well before letting them drop on the ground for a third time. Each nut fell and rolled into position, exactly the same as before.

The old woman studied the nuts for a moment longer. Then she looked up. "Tell the Ogiso that his misfortunes are caused by a witch among his wives," she said slowly. The chiefs leaned forward as the old woman talked. She went on, "Tell the Ogiso that she has to be destroyed before the cloud of his misfortunes will be removed."

"But how will we know who she is?" asked the chiefs.

"It is the one they call Esago," the old woman replied, rising slowly, "She must be destroyed." With that, the old woman stood up and left. The chiefs remained sitting for a while, barely able to understand what they had just been told.

Esago gathered the nuts and flung them viciously against the walls of the shrine. "It is a lie!" she cried angrily, "Don't you see, it is all a lie!"

The chiefs hurried back to Benin, intent on delivering their message. Esago tried everything she could think of to try to persuade them to change the message, but to no avail. The chiefs were no longer interested in anything Esago had to say. They had only one thought on their minds, to tell the Osigo exactly what the Oracle had told them.

As they neared Benin, Esago became more and more worried. Nothing she said made any difference. She had tried pleading with the chiefs, she had tried threatening them, but still they insisted on delivering their message. Finally Esago thought of a plan. She brought out some magic powder, spoke a few secret words and blew the fine dust into the faces of the two men.

Esago had cast a spell, and the chiefs were now hypnotized. Esago the witch made the chiefs recite the message that she decided the Ogiso should hear. When she was satisfied that they would do what she told them, she ordered them to hurry on to Benin.

The chiefs went to the palace and sought an immediate audience with the Ogiso. They bowed humbly before their ruler. "What news from the Oracle?" the Ogiso asked.

"Your Majesty, we have bad news," they replied. Esago was lurking furtively in a corner, listening to every word. The chiefs then went on, "The gods require a sacrifice."

"Anything to please the gods. I will order it immediately," Owodo answered.

"Your Majesty, the news is not good - you don't understand. The sacrifice the gods require is not a goat or a cow. It is not even a slave, Your Majesty."

"Then what is it?" Owodo asked, the cold hand of fear clutching at his heart.

"Your son, Ekaladeran," they replied in unison.

"My son?" Owodo repeated in shock...

Owodo paced about in his private chambers all day and night. He refused to see anybody and would not eat. In the small hours of the morning Esago came into the room. "What am I to do, Esago?" he asked his favourite wife.

Esago pretended to think for a moment. Then she said, "He who disobeys the gods courts disaster. We must do as the Oracle has spoken."

"But he is my only son, a mere child," Owodo exclaimed helplessly.

Esago smiled secretly, inwardly sensing victory. She had never liked the boy. The fact that the gods had not seen fit to give her a son was enough reason for her to hate Ekaladeran. "Think of it not as losing a son but of gaining several offspring. That is after all what you want, what we all want." she purred evilly.

The next day Owodo called for the executioners. He reluctantly gave the order for his only son to be slain.

In the early hours of the morning, before the first cock had crowed, Ekaladeran was rudely awoken from his sleep and made to dress quickly. "What is the matter?" he asked again and again as he pulled on his clothes and rubbed his sleepy eyes. But the only reply the attendants gave was to urge him to hurry.

Under the cover of darkness, Ekaladeran was led out of the palace grounds to a place where two men were waiting to receive him. Ekaladeran was introduced to the men and told that they were taking him on a long journey.

After a hurried goodbye, his escorts went back towards the palace while Ekaladeran followed the two men. They walked deeper and deeper into the forest. The sun began to rise high in the sky, and soon its heat was beating down on the forest. Ekaladeran was tired and hungry. "Are we almost there?" he asked impatiently. The two executioners were walking a little way ahead of the boy, whispering intently to each other.

The forest of the tropics may be thick and dense but it hides few secrets. Everywhere there are whispers carried by the trees to the animals, by the birds of prey who see what should remain hidden, by the wind that hears what it should not. We will never know how the executioners found out the true story. But they had, and that hot, early morning, as they took the boy deeper and deeper into the forest, they discussed among themselves the great injustice that killing Ekaladeran would be.

Ekaladeran's childish voice rang through the forest once again. "I'm tired. I want to go home."

The executioners turned to Ekaladeran and sat him on the root of an iroko tree. "Do you know who we are?" they asked.

Ekaladeran nodded. "You are servants of my father."

The executioners exchanged a glance. "Not the sort of servants you think," muttered one.

For a moment there was awkwardness. The executioners took in the boy's big brown eyes, the smooth roundness of his face untouched by the harsh hands of age. He was only a boy, his limbs long and skinny. Would he understand? they wondered. Yet for his sake, the sake of their country, he had to. He was, after all, the only heir to the throne of Benin.

And so they sat with Ekaladeran and for several hours talked, each in turn. They began by telling the boy the reason for their journey. Ekaladeran listened, disbelief, fear and then anger masking his face as they told him all about the Ogiso's order to have him killed as a sacrifice so that his other wives would bear him children. They told him about the rumours which claimed that Esago was a witch and how it was secretly believed that she was responsible for all the troubles in the kingdom. They also told the boy of the people's increasing dissatisfaction with their weak and easily manipulated ruler.

Finally, they told Ekaladeran that they had decided not to carry out the Ogiso's instructions - they would let him go. Ekaladeran thanked his liberators, picked up his only possession, a catapult, and wandered away into the forest.

Unlike his weak and cowardly father, Ekaladeran had the heart of a lion. He was as courageous as he was fearless. He was determined that, if it was his father's wish to deny his birthright,

he would seek his fortune elsewhere. As the forest closed behind him, not once did he look back towards Benin.

After Ekaladeran had gone, the executioners caught a chicken and killed it. They rubbed its blood on their sword and took this back to the Ogiso to confirm that they had carried out the task. The Ogiso saw the sword caked with blood and believed that Ekaladeran was dead...

Years passed. Owodo was getting old and so were his wives. To his increasing alarm, none of them had yet given birth. The thought that he had sacrificed the only child the gods were willing to bless him with, and that it had all been in vain, tortured him. Daily, Owodo wept at his misfortune. He withdrew into himself and performed fewer and fewer of the functions required of a ruler.

The country was becoming more and more unsettled as people made known their dissatisfaction with their ruler. Daily, reports reached Owodo of rallies and gatherings at which people publicly denounced Owodo. People were asking uncomfortable questions. They wondered why the Ogiso had allowed his only son to be killed. Why Benin was without an heir to the throne. Rumours were rife - it was said Owodo was weak because he had allowed himself to be manipulated by his wives.

Meanwhile, Esago was desperately trying to hang on to her position as favourite wife. This was proving difficult because Owodo had stopped confiding in her. After he had followed her advice and allowed Ekaladeran to be sacrificed to no avail, he quite simply lost interest in her. No longer did he welcome her into his private rooms. He treated her almost as a forgotten wife.

With Owodo turning against her, Esago fast realized that she had no allies. She had never made friends with the other wives, who now watched her gradually diminishing status with glee. Most unsettling were the whispers which were filtering through the palace walls implying that she was a witch. Esago lived with the fear that these rumours would one day reach the Ogiso's ears.

One day, Owodo was in his council chamber, presiding over matters of state. The most senior chiefs in the land described the grave misgivings that they had about the state of the country. They feared that if something was not done immediately, there would be a serious uprising that threatened to destroy the monarchy. Owodo only half-listened. Matters of state had not much interested him anyway. It was usually his prime minister, the Iyase, who dealt with such serious issues. Absent-mindedly, Owodo wondered where the Iyase was. It was quite unlike him to miss a meeting of this importance.

At that very moment, the Iyase burst into the room. He was a stout, stocky man with an air of authority that had always impressed Owodo. As he made his way towards the throne, Owodo thought it was most unlike the Iyase to be so excitable.

"Your Majesty," the Iyase lay on the ground respectfully before the monarch.

Owodo replied in an appropriate manner.

"We must talk, Your Majesty. I have news..."

Owodo pointed to the chiefs who had now stopped the meeting and were looking curiously at the Iyase. The Iyase turned and bowed respectfully to the chiefs before turning back to Owodo. "It is most important, Your Majesty."

Owodo thought for a short moment. "Very well," he said. With a flick of his fly-switch he dismissed the meeting. The chiefs rose. Bowing politely before Owodo, they filed out of the room. Soon the chamber was empty except for the Iyase, Owodo and his two sword-bearers.

"So what is so important that you had to miss a meeting?" Owodo asked casually.

"Your Majesty, I have the most incredible news. It appears that your son Ekaladeran was not killed all those years ago."

The fly-switch dropped from Owodo's hand. He appeared to be in shock, staring speechlessly at his senior minister.

The man nodded vigorously, happy to be the one to be imparting this good news to the Ogiso. "Yes, Your Majesty, it is the most amazing information. I think this will solve all our problems."

"But can it be true?" Owodo wondered, "How do we know he is really Ekaladeran?"

The Iyase gave an order to a sword-bearer. He went to the door of the council chamber and came back with the two executioners. They prostrated themselves before Owodo, their faces masks of fear.

"These are the men you gave the task of killing Ekaladeran," the Iyase said by way of introduction.

Owodo peered closely at the two elderly men. He remembered them from all those years ago. He even remembered the blood-caked sword they brought back to show him that they had carried out the deed.

"So you lied - you did not kill him?" Owodo asked slowly.

The two men fell to the ground, trembling with fear. Owodo looked down at them. "Tell me everything," he commanded.

And so, at long last the secret was out. The executioners were now old men. Age had driven away some of their fears and misgivings. They stood before the Ogiso and told him that they had taken the decision themselves not to kill Ekaladeran because they felt it would have been a great injustice. They talked and Owodo listened. Then there was silence.

"And so you decided to let him go?" Owodo said finally.

"Yes, Your Majesty."

"But the blood...you showed me blood...on your sword," Owodo said puzzled.

"Only the blood of a chicken, Your Majesty," the men replied.

Owodo sat back and thought. He felt that the gods were giving him one last chance. In a sudden rush of generosity, he dismissed the executioners and ordered that they should be well rewarded.

Many miles away, at a neighbouring town called Ughoton, Ekaladeran, now a handsome young man, had made his home and was on his way to making his fortune. Time had been kind to him, and he was now a successful and popular market trader.

Owodo wanted his son back in Benin immediately, by his side. He had never had the opportunity to tell him the things a father tells to a son. He had missed seeing his only son grow into manhood. He was determined that he would waste no more time, so he ordered warriors to go to Ughoton and capture Ekaladeran.

When Esago heard that Ekaladeran was still alive, she was terrified that her secret was finally out. She ran into the thick forests looking for a place to hide, but the forests would not hide her. The wind carried her scent to the wild animals who sought her out and devoured her.

Ekaladeran was a very popular trader at Ughoton. News reached him that warriors from Benin had been sent to capture him and take him back to the city. Ekaladeran had no desire to return or be returned to Benin. He and his close friends took a few of their possessions and ran into the forest. The soldiers reached Ughoton and were told that Ekaladeran was no longer there. They returned to Benin empty-handed.

Ekaladeran and his friends trekked for weeks through the thick forests. Eventually they came to a place that was peaceful. The people were friendly and welcomed them kindly. Ekaladeran felt that this was a place where he would find peace. So he and his friends decided to settle in this place, which was called Ile-Ife. Soon Ekaladeran began to trade again.

The years passed. Ekaladeran became very rich. He married and had many children.

Meanwhile, back in Benin, things were getting worse. Owodo was fast becoming more and more unpopular. There were open revolts against the monarchy. Owodo was aging and there was no one to succeed him. He quickly sank into deep depression. He had completely divorced himself from all matters of state. The country was now effectively run by Iyase and the senior chiefs.

Several more years passed. News again reached Owodo, now an old, unhappy man, that Ekaladeran was a rich man, living in Ile-Ife. This time, Owodo sent chiefs to the country to beg Ekaladeran to return to Benin. But Ekaladeran was not interested in leaving Ile-Ife. He told the chiefs that he was comfortable as he was - he had wealth, property, wives and children, and he could not leave it all to return to Benin. So the chiefs went back to Benin to tell the dispirited ruler that Ekaladeran would not come.

Soon after, things deteriorated in Benin so much that Owodo was banished for bad government. He died in exile, alone and miserable, destined never to see his only son again.

Oba Ohen

Oba Ohen came to the throne in 1334 AD. When he was young, he was a handsome and intelligent man, but it is said that a misfortune befell him in the twentieth year of his reign. This is his story...

Oba Ohen was a powerful Benin ruler who lived a long, long time ago. In those days Benin was a formidable and important empire that enjoyed the respect of all its neighbouring states. It was not uncommon for rulers from other towns to pay their respects by sending the Oba lavish presents of coral beads, fine cloth or livestock. Often performers from neighbouring villages would seek permission to show their high regard for the Oba by performing at his court.

A very famous performer lived at Uta which was a small village on the outskirts of Benin. Every year this man and his entourage would go to the court of Benin to perform before the Oba. It soon became an event to which people looked forward each year. The performer was a skilled dancer and acrobat. His performances always attracted huge audiences.

This year's performance had created the usual excitement. People turned out in large numbers to watch in the huge, open courtyard at the front of the palace. The Oba took his place on a magnificent bronze throne, flanked by his numerous courtiers and attendants. When the Oba gave the order, the performance began. People whooped with delight as the performer began a slow dance, interpreting the rhythms of the ukose which his wife played with simple grace.

People cheered as the performer went into his next routine. The musicians joined in and the tempo increased. The music and the performer were as one. Soon, he began the acrobatic displays for which he was justly famous. The crowd cheered as he thrilled them with feats of agility and skill.

It seemed that the performer had succeeded in mesmerizing all his audience. All, except the Oba who stared with a strange, distant look at the beautiful wife of the performer. In fact, the Oba could not take his eyes off her. Never had he seen a woman more beautiful or with as much grace. She danced by her husband as she played the ukose, her body moving in perfect time to the music.

After the performance, it was the custom for the performer to come forward and stand before the Oba who would then reward him with money. The amount would depend on how much the performer had succeeded in pleasing the Oba. Oba Ohen gave this performer a generous sum of money, but then, breaking with tradition, he asked for the performer's wife to come forward. He instructed his servants to give her more money than had been given to the performer. The woman, though a little surprised, accepted the money graciously. The performer hid his displeasure and thanked the Oba for his generosity.

Days later, the Oba still could not get the performer's wife out of his mind. He thought about her morning, noon and night. Finally, he sent some messengers to find out where she lived.

One night, Oba Ohen made a secret visit to the home of the woman at Ute with only a few of his most trusted servants. He told his servants to stand watch in the bushes while he crept up to the woman's room and knocked on the door. "Who is it?" called the woman. When she opened the door, she was shocked at who was there. "Your Majesty..." she began, unsure what to say next.

"I must talk to you," the Oba pleaded in a most undignified manner, "please let me in."

The woman realized that the Oba was desperately uneasy. But then her mind flashed to her husband. She was terrified of annoying him, for it was no secret that he had a very powerful juju. "I'm sorry, Your Majesty, but my husband would kill me if he knew," she replied.

"I will prevent any harm from coming to you," the Oba said, "Let me in only for a moment. I can't keep standing out here. You never know who may be listening."

The woman looked out into the harsh darkness of the night and shivered. "Very well then," she said as she reluctantly opened the door wider to allow the Oba to enter her room.

Once inside, Oba Ohen held the woman's hands and gazed earnestly at her delicate yet perfect features. Her skin glowed, without a single blemish. Her eyes were the most magnetic he had ever seen. As he stared into them, he felt himself falling even more deeply in love with this vision of loveliness. Oba Ohen began to plead with the woman to come and live with him in his palace as one of his wives. He told her he would compensate her husband well and buy her everything she ever dreamed of. The woman listened, fascinated at the lavish world the Oba described to her.

Meanwhile, the performer was relaxing in his living-room. In those days, families lived in large compounds. The head of the house, usually the husband, would live in a large house in the centre of the compound. His wives would have smaller houses dotted round the main house. The performer suddenly started to feel a prickly sensation all over his body, Great magician that he was, he recognized the signs immediately - there was a trespasser on his compound. He went into his bedroom and picked up a walking-stick. Then he made the short journey round his compound. It was when he was standing outside his beautiful young wife's house that the prickly sensation was strongest. He knew then that she was entertaining a guest.

Oba Ohen's servants who were hidden in the bushes had soon been lulled to sleep as they drank in the heady scent of the soft grasses and were caressed by the gentle night breezes. And so they failed to spot the performer. A sudden loud knock on the door startled the young woman. "My husband!" she exclaimed, "He mustn't find us here like this - you must hide." She looked around the little room, but there was nowhere to hide. Finally she told the Oba to get onto the bed and pulled the sheets over him.

The knocking sounded again. "Open this door!" called the performer.

The young woman called out, "Not now, I am unwell, a little later perhaps."

The performer replied with an even harder bang on the door. "Open this door now, or I will break it down," he commanded.

His wife cried out desperately, "I beg you to let me be. I really *cannot* see you now." She looked towards the door. There was complete silence. She stood there for a moment longer. Still silence. The Oba peeped out of the sheets. Their eyes met. They started to believe that the performer had given

up and left when a sudden almighty bang shattered the
wooden door into several jagged pieces. The woman screamed
as her husband rushed into the room, his face an angry mask.
He stood for a moment and looked round the tiny room. Then
pushing his wife roughly out of the way, he strode to the bed.

The frightened woman sank to the ground in a corner of the room, too terrified to watch what would happen next.

The performer took in the obvious lump beneath the sheets. "I don't care to know who you are," he growled. Then raising his walking-stick, he smashed it down on the body several times. There was not one yell from the Oba who with a superhuman will managed to keep dead still. Suddenly, in a very abrupt manner, the performer turned and left the room.

The wife rushed up to the bed. She pulled back the covers and saw the Oba grimacing with pain. The commotion had awoken his servants who rushed into the little house to see what the trouble was. They found the Oba shaking in agony. On closer examination it was revealed that both his legs were broken. The Oba was carried back to the palace on a stretcher.

The next few months were very troubled ones for Oba Ohen. It became clear that the damage done to his legs was severe. In fact, he could no longer walk. In the greatest secrecy, the best and most powerful healers, medicine men and physicians were summoned to the palace. But none could cure the Oba's condition.

Oba Ohen became increasingly worried. In Benin, the Oba was regarded as a god. He was worshipped by the people. He was the earthly representation of physical, moral and spiritual perfection. A lame Oba would destroy the myth. It might cause people to question the Oba's claim to physical superiority and hence erode his power. Oba Ohen realized that, this time, his recklessness had landed him in a serious mess.

From then on, Oba Ohen's personality changed. No longer did he rule Benin with the restraint and confidence that had marked his earlier years. He was now a frightened, lonely man, and it showed in the strange behaviour which marked the last remaining years of his reign. Oba Ohen began to neglect his official duties. He refused to leave the palace and was no longer interested in receiving visitors.

Not surprisingly, people noticed the changes in their Oba. One such person was Iyase Emuze. Next to the Oba, he was the most important man in the city. He was the Oba's closest adviser, his role similar to that of a prime minister. Normally, he had free access to come and go from the palace as often as he wished. It was usual for him to be granted an audience with the Oba daily as there were always matters of state which had to be discussed.

Oba Ohen retreated more and more into himself. He became suspicious of everyone. The Iyase's bright and cheerful demeanour only served to make the Oba more resentful and suspicious of his motives. Finally, he told his servants to tell the Iyase that he was no longer welcome in his private rooms. No longer would it be necessary for him to seek a daily audience as Oba Ohen now intended to restrict their meetings to public ceremonies.

When Iyase Emuze received this message, he was perturbed. That was no way to rule a country, he thought. To be shut in your palace and not receive outsiders, not even your closest advisers. What exactly was wrong with the Oba? he wondered as he thought over some of the strange things that Ohen had done lately.

There was the business of official ceremonies. It was the custom for the Oba to arrive last and to leave first. Oba Ohen had changed things. He had recently ordered that he should arrive first and leave last. The Iyase did not know then that this was in order to allow Oba Ohen to hide his lameness. The Oba was carried into the hall by his trusted servants who arranged his robes so that they hid his distorted legs, and he was carried out again after everyone had left. The Iyase thought the Oba's behaviour was most peculiar.

Then there was the business of visitors. The Oba now refused to receive guests, even the important delegates from distant and important lands. This was causing more than just embarrassment to those who had to explain to the foreign visitors why the Oba could not receive them. It was also causing people to lose respect for Benin. And now this latest message, the Iyase mused, well aware of the rumours that had been spreading among the people. Some said that the Oba was ill, others that he was possessed. Everyone agreed that their Oba was a changed man. Fights broke out in the city between the people who still supported the Oba and those who felt that he was no longer fit to govern. Iyase Emuze realized that something had to be done soon before there was a complete breakdown of law and order. He was determined to find out what had caused the change in the Oba's behaviour.

Emuze's sister was one of the Oba's wives. Royal wives were confined to special quarters and guarded by loyal servants. The wives could only talk to other men when they were in the main part of the palace and from a distance of several yards.

So when Emuze crept up to his sister and whispered in her ear, she was alarmed. It was most unlike her brother to break palace rules. But she listened to him. The following day she turned up at the secret place where Iyase Emuze had asked to meet her. Emuze asked her if she knew of any reason which could account for the Oba's recent strange behaviour.

But his sister kept silent. She knew what had happened to the Oba, as did all his other wives, but they had been made to swear on the Oba's juju never to tell another living soul. The punishment for breaking her promise was instant death. So she kept silent. But, back in her private chamber, she wondered what to do. She knew that what was going on could not continue. Something had to be done. She believed that if there was one person who could do anything it had to be her brother, so she desperately wanted him to know the truth. If she could not say what had happened to the Oba because of her promise, then perhaps there was another way of letting him know...

She summoned a servant to bring her a dead cockerel. When the servant had left, she broke both the cockerel's legs and put it in a box, wrapped it up and sent it to her brother, through her personal maid. Emuze received this odd gift. Things, he thought, were getting stranger and stranger. He was more determined than ever to get to the bottom of it all.

A few days later, the Iyase attended a state meeting in the council chamber. The room was large and impressive. Bronze plaques depicting historical events lined the walls. The Oba's throne was on a raised platform at one end of the hall. As had become usual, Emuze entered the council chamber to find the Oba already waiting to start the meeting. The senior chiefs filed in, paid their respects to the Oba and took their seats.

After the meeting, the chiefs paid their respects to the Oba once more and left the council chamber. Iyase Emuze rose last, reluctant to leave. Oba Ohen called out good-naturedly, "Iyase, are you not going home tonight, or should we all sleep here?" The Iyase laughed politely. He rose from his seat, said good night to the Oba and walked out of the council chamber. But instead of going straight along the corridor and out to the courtyard, he followed the corridor round to the back of the hall.

Iyase Emuze saw two large, bronze vases covered with cowhide next to the private door through which the Oba used to enter and leave the council chamber. Emuze had an idea.

Lifting the skin off one of the vases, he climbed into it. Then he pulled the lid back over the vase and waited.

It was cramped in the vase and Emuze, who was not a small man, began to feel very uncomfortable after a short while. He shifted and tried to relieve the pressure on his limbs, but the blood still drained from his legs, keeping his face locked in a grimace of pain. As the minutes ticked by, Emuze began to wonder if perhaps this was such a good idea. There was no way he could keep this up for much longer. He had begun to contemplate leaving when a sudden noise caught his attention. Emuze recognised it immediately. It was the great doors at the back of the council chamber being opened.

Emuze stiffened and listened. He heard a rush of footsteps as attendants entered the inner hall. They gave the order that all was clear. Emuze lifted the lid of the vase slightly and peeped out. From where he hid, he could clearly see everything. The Oba was brought into the hall, carried on a seat by two guards. Two others walked behind him carrying his robes. Emuze's eyes were drawn to the legs of the Oba dangling uselessly beneath him. Emuze gave a gasp of surprise.

At that moment, the cowhide lid was torn from the vase. Emuze found himself blinking into the face of a royal attendant.

Emuze was unceremoniously dragged from his hiding-place, both his arms securely held by guards.

"Why do you have to sneak up on me, Emuze?" the Oba demanded.

"Your Majesty..." Emuze began, confused and disturbed at what he had seen, "The people have a right to know..."

"And who gives the people their rights?" the Oba shouted, "Am I not the Oba? Am I not to be respected? Why have you disobeyed my wishes?"

Emuze suddenly realized that the Oba was mad, stark raving mad.

"What will you do with me?" he asked softly.

Oba Ohen looked at Emuze with burning eyes. "If I let you go, you will run around the city and talk like a parrot," he said, gesticulating wildly. "Kill him," he instructed the guards.

"You will not get away with this," Emuze yelled as he was led away. "The people have a right to know...they will know eventually, believe me."

117

And that was the last that was ever seen of Iyase Emuze...

The next morning Emuze's wife rushed to the palace with her only child. She burst into the council chamber and began to tell the Oba that her husband had failed to come home the night before. She was worried sick. With an air of complete disinterest, the Oba turned to his attendants. "Remove this stupid, babbling woman from my presence," he said. Hurt and confused, she left the palace and went to the homes of the seven Councillors of State.

When the Councillors of State (the most senior chiefs in the land) heard about Emuze's disappearance, they were very worried. They had all been at the council chamber with Emuze and the Oba the previous night. They clearly remembered that Emuze had waited behind at the palace when the meeting was over. They found it disturbing to hear how the Oba had reacted to the news of the disappearance of Emuze. After all, not only was he the Oba's chief minister, they were supposed to be close friends.

The chiefs decided to mount a major investigation to find out what had happened to Emuze. They began to question everyone who had been at the palace that evening. Oba Ohen's increasingly unpleasant behaviour had made him many enemies, not just outside the palace, but also within. And so, as the investigation gathered pace, the chiefs found people willing to talk. They eventually found out the truth about what had happened to Emuze that night from the mouths of the people who had actually carried out the execution.

The chiefs were horrified at what they had uncovered. They retired to a safe place to discuss what to do. As they talked, the terrifying significance of the Oba's reckless actions became clearer. "If he can kill the highest chief in the land, Iyase Emuze, if he can do that to him, he could do the same to any one of us," they said, "Perhaps that is his plan. Perhaps he wants to kill us off one by one."

All agreed that their lives were no longer safe and that, this time, Oba Ohen had gone way too far. "He must go," they said, knowing that in Benin, death was the only way to remove an Oba.

It took three years for the chiefs to plan the Oba's death. Under their instructions, men were secretly smuggled into the palace. The men entered the council chamber and dug a deep hole which they covered with weak planks of wood. They then covered these with a white cloth as they had been instructed to do. The throne was put back in its place over the hole, so everything looked normal again.

The chiefs waited until there was an occasion which would require the Oba's presence. It came a few weeks later. The celebration was a festival in honour of the Oba's ancestors.

As was now usual, the Oba was brought out to the council chamber before anyone arrived. He took his place on the throne which stood over the white cloth. No one heard the faint creaking noise as Oba Ohen adjusted himself so that his robes covered his legs.

Soon the hall filled up. The chiefs stood around the throne in their flowing ceremonial robes. Unknown to the Oba or his attendants, each man had armed himself with a lump of white chalk.

Before the ceremony proceeded, one of the chiefs called Bagua stood before the Oba and, pointing to the place Iyase Emuze would have stood, asked with his eyes and a gesture of his hands, "Where is Iyase Emuze?"

The Oba replied by shaking his head, shrugging his shoulders and raising his hands. I don't know, was the unspoken reply.

Bagua then gave the order. The chiefs stepped forward, pressure was placed on the throne, and suddenly the already weak planks broke and crashed down into the pit, carrying the Oba and his throne down with them. The chiefs brought out their lumps of chalk and stoned the Oba to death.

And as he died, they sang:

Ohen, take chalk!

So that you may go!

Oba Ohen had ruled for 36 years when he was killed. White chalk was traditionally used to honour dead kings in their graves. It became the weapon for ending Oba Ohen's life.

The Fugitive Prince

In 1440 AD Ewuare the Great came to the throne. He is generally regarded as the greatest ruler ever in Benin. But the road to the throne was far from smooth for this remarkable young man who was known as Prince Ogun before he came to the throne.

In the previous story, we saw how Oba Ohen met his death. He left four sons. By the time Egbeka, the eldest of Ohen's sons, came to the throne, Benin had become a troubled place. The palace chiefs were now very powerful, and the young Oba was unable to control them. Egbeka did not live very long, neither did his brother Orobiru, as fights broke out between the people who had supported Oba Ohen and those who had played a part in his death. The chiefs and nobles took advantage of the confusion in the kingdom to increase their own powers.

The situation in the kingdom of Benin continued to get worse. Prince Ogun, Oba Ohen's third son, who was now the next in line to the throne after the deaths of his two elder brothers, heard disturbing rumours. It was said that the chiefs were planning to get rid of the monarchy once and for all. The prince heard that there were people who plotted to kill him as they had killed his father. Prince Ogun became increasingly more fearful for his life and eventually, he decided to flee the city.

One night, he did so, taking his younger brother Prince Irughe with him. The two young men stole out of Benin and took refuge in the vast forests that surrounded the city. Prince Ogun had began his seven year exile...

Life in the forest was hard. The two princes were not accustomed to sleeping rough under the stars, with the hard earth for a bed. They had not learned the hunter's skills, so they found it difficult to catch many animals to eat. They had not learned about the roots and fruits, so they could not easily distinguish the poisonous from the edible. After a short while, Prince Ogun began to miss home. He wished desperately to return, but feared for his life.

One night, as the two brothers were sitting round a small fire, roasting the single plantain which was the only food they had managed to find all day, Prince Ogun began to talk about home.

"Do you think that there are people who miss us?" he asked. Irughe shrugged and kept silent. "There must be," Prince Ogun mused on, "I know that there are still people left who are loyal to the throne."

"Look what you are doing!" Prince Irughe shouted suddenly. It was too late. The plantain, which Ogun had attached to a stick and was holding over the fire, had fallen in. Ogun watched in barely comprehending shock as the plantain caught fire and began to burn. Then his reflexes took over. He plunged the stick into the fire in a desperate bid to save their supper. But when he eventually managed to toss the plantain out of the fire, the pale orange flesh had been reduced to a black, charred mass, no good for anything.

Prince Ogun looked up at his brother who was staring down

balefully at the plantain. Ogun knew what Irughe was thinking because he was thinking exactly the same thing. How could it happen? How could life be so cruel? The only thing they had found to eat all day, and this had to happen.

"I can't take this any more," Irughe said, going to sit under a large tree.

Ogun watched him for a moment. Then he put out the fire and tossed what should have been their supper into the long grass. He went to sit by his brother. There was silence for a while. Ogun could hear the deep, angry growls of his stomach mingling with the sounds of the forest at night. He looked up at his brother. "You know, Irughe, I've been thinking. Perhaps you should return."

At this Irughe looked up, but he did not say a word.

"I was the one they were plotting against, not you. I am sure the chiefs could not justify killing you," Ogun continued.

After a long moment, in which Irughe took time to consider what his brother was saying, he replied softly, "Perhaps I will."

"Go back to Benin. If everything is all right, then send for me," Ogun stated simply.

"All right," Irughe nodded, looking up at his brother. Ogun noticed that, almost miraculously, the stress of the past few weeks, which had etched deep lines of worry into the younger man's face, seemed to have lifted.

The two brothers talked far into the night. Ogun reflected on the things he would do if he ever became Oba. "First, I'd call myself Uwaifiokun, meaning 'There's always plenty'. Then I would make sure that nobody ever went hungry again."

"There'd be plantains for all," Irughe chimed in.

"Sacks and sacks and sacks of plantains for everybody," Ogun chorused. Both brothers laughed and continued chatting until the first rays of dawn filtered through the canopy of leaves above.

A few hours later, Ogun escorted his brother a short distance. Then it was time to part. Ogun hugged his younger brother and gazed deeply into his face. "Take care of yourself," he whispered in a voice full of emotion.

"I will come back for you, brother, I will come back," Irughe promised. One more hug and then he was gone, beating a path through the thick of the forest, soon to be hidden by the foliage.

Ogun stared after his brother for a few more moments. He uttered a silent prayer to the ancestors, asking them to look kindly upon Irughe. Then he picked up his spear and his small bundle of possessions and headed in whichever direction destiny would lead him.

Ogun missed his brother almost immediately. He missed the idle chatter they shared, he missed the companionship and, most of all, he missed having someone to lean on when he was down. But he knew that the time was not right for him to return to Benin. Ogun accepted his fate and carried on his lonely journey. Several hours later, he reached a place that was cool and calm. He heard the tranquil sounds of trickling water and parted the bushes to reveal a stream making its unhurried journey.

As Ogun knelt by the banks of the water to wash his face, he heard a shrill cry. Looking up, he saw a large bird perched on top of a tree to his left. Slowly, Ogun pulled his spear from its sheath. He took aim and flung the spear with all his might. The loud, angry call of the bird convinced Ogun that he had hit his target. He waited for the bird to drop, but, to his surprise, it stretched its large wings and with a sudden flutter flew away, high over the treetops, the spear sticking into its back like a grotesque third wing.

Ogun continued to stare after the bird long after it had disappeared from sight. He could not believe what had just happened. Convinced that it was a bad omen, he decided to hunt for the bird and retrieve his spear. So he picked up his small bundle of possessions and walked in the direction the bird had flown.

Several hours later, night was waiting impatiently to claim the earth. Ogun had just begun to give up hope of ever finding the bird or his spear when he saw a large boa constrictor at the foot of a tree. Standing quite still in his tracks, he watched the creature swallow the last of its meal. Ogun crept closer as the snake uncurled itself and wriggled. Then he noticed that half of the body of the snake covered an object which he recognised immediately as his spear. Ogun wondered how to retrieve his weapon. A creature that large could crush him in an instant. He realized that it would be too dangerous to confront it just yet, so he decided to wait, hoping that soon the creature would fall asleep.

Eventually, Ogun's patience was rewarded. The snake stopped writhing and squirming, arranged its body into several large coils, and was still. Ogun continued to watch. When, several minutes later, there was no sign of movement from the creature, he picked up a rock and crept up to it. Then he lifted the rock high above his head and let it fall.

The rock smashed down on the head of the snake, breaking the skin and crushing the bone beneath. As Ogun watched, the snake lifted its head in a slow, agonized circle and opened its large, toothless mouth. It had uncurled itself and its head moved towards Ogun who stumbled back a few feet, stopping when he realized that his path was blocked by a tree. He stood, numb with fear, staring at the snake which inched closer and closer.

Ogun looked around hurriedly for a weapon, grasping at the roots of the tree, but there was nothing that would come away in his hand. From deep within the creature came a loud, rasping hiss. Then it seemed to retch. Ogun watched as several small shiny stones fell from its mouth. The creature retched once more, and then was still.

Ogun circled the snake carefully, once, then twice. It was still, completely unmoving. He took a stone and threw it at the creature's head. Still there was no movement. Finally, Ogun stepped forward and retrieved his spear. He picked up a few of the pebbles which the snake had vomited up. Looking at them closely, he discovered they were precious stones. Ogun filled his pockets, then left the snake where it lay.

Ogun walked a short distance before reaching a place where he decided he would spend the night. His meal was meagre, just some fruit which he had plucked along the way. Clutching his precious spear, he fell asleep under a large iroko tree.

Ogun slept deeply, lost in a dreamless world. He was awoken by the cries of an ibis. He rubbed his heavy eyes, then became aware of liquid dripping on his head. He looked up and sprang to his feet. For, sitting on a branch, just above where he had slept was a leopard which had just finished devouring its prey. From its mouth and nose dripped the blood of the animal it had eaten. Ogun flung his spear at the beast and watched as it came tumbling down, smashing into the undergrowth.

Is this a sign from the ancestors? Ogun wondered, convinced that it was their way of telling him not to give up hope, their way of letting him know that one day he would wear the crown. He would be Oba of Benin...

Meanwhile, back in Benin, things had rapidly gone from bad to worse. There was a complete breakdown of law and order. The chiefs who had taken the laws into their own hands found it increasingly impossible to govern. Wars and famines claimed many lives. When, in desperation, the senior chiefs went to the Oracle to find out what they must do to restore Benin to normality, they were told that it was the will of the ancestors that the rightful heir be placed on the throne. So the chiefs sent out search parties to find Prince Ogun or, in the event of his death, his brother Prince Irughe.

At about this time, Prince Irughe arrived on the outskirts of Benin. He was tired and hungry from his journey. His clothes were tattered and dirty. Irughe found the place as he had left it, peacefully rural. Women came and went with their water vessels on their heads. Children played in the sand, their bare feet stirring up the red Benin earth. Men gathered under the shade of trees, drinking palm wine and gossiping.

Irughe walked cautiously through the streets, but no one paid him any attention. To the casual observer he was simply a poor tramp. Then he came across an old woman fetching water from a well. She was alone. Irughe watched her for a while. Her movements were slow and laboured. With quiet deliberation she pulled the rope that would bring the bucket of water to the surface. Then she carefully lifted the bucket and poured the contents into her own container which stood by the edge of the well. Her movements were not very steady, so she succeeded in pouring more of the water on the ground than into her bowl.

Finally, she let go of the bucket and bent to lift the bowl up onto her head, but her limbs were old and stiff. Irughe could hear the painful creaking of joints as the woman continued her arduous task. He crept out from his hiding-place.

"Ma, let me..."

As his shadow fell across her path, the woman stiffened. At the sound of his voice she jumped. When she had straightened herself enough to look at him, she let out a slight scream, thinking the dirty, haggard, unshaven person who stood before her could only be a thief, or worse...

"Ma, do not be afraid - I will not harm you," Irughe promised, reading the fear in her eyes.

"What do you want?" the woman cackled, words coming from a toothless mouth.

"Do not be afraid...here, let me help." With that, Irughe attempted to carry the bowl of water but was stopped by the woman. She continued to look at him, still suspicious. Then she seemed to see something in his face, beneath the weeks of grime and the untidy stubble, which made her pause and bend closer.

"Are you not...but you are...it is you...Prince...Prince Irughe?" she whispered, waving a bony finger in his face.

Irughe nodded doubtfully. Now that she knew, what would she do? he wondered. She continued to look critically into his face for a moment longer and then a smile lit up her wrinkly, old face.

"It is you, the son of our late Oba, welcome, welcome," she said respectfully and happily.

Irughe's relief knew no bounds. That she greeted him with such warmth meant one thing - she was on his side.

"Come, my son, you need a bath, you need food, shelter." So saying, she led him to her meagre home.

When Irughe had washed and eaten, he began to talk to the old woman. The questions came tumbling out. The old woman answered as best as she could. She told the young prince about the terrible turmoil that had fallen on Benin, about the message from the Oracle which stated that, unless the rightful heir to the throne was crowned, Benin would not be at peace. "So the throne remains vacant. Even as we speak, the search parties are out looking for you and Prince Ogun."

That night, Prince Irughe lay on a bed for the first time in several months. But even though the room was cool and the bed comfortable, he could not sleep. His mind was busy as he thought over the implication of the things the old woman had told him.

The next morning, he thanked the old woman for her hospitality and left after a hearty meal. Once in the main part of the city, there were many more people about in the streets. It was not long before he was recognised. People rushed to greet him, others to escort him to the palace. News of his arrival reached the chiefs in their homes who made hurried preparations to go to the palace.

"Where is Prince Ogun?" was the question on everyone's lips.

"My poor brother is dead," Irughe replied every time he was asked the question. "My unfortunate brother was devoured by the beasts of the forest."

Meetings were held. The priests met, the chiefs met, the nobles met, and all discussed the implications of what Irughe had told them. If Ogun was dead, Irughe had become the rightful heir to the throne.

Benin was still in a troubled state. The kingmakers wanted to go ahead and crown Irughe as soon as possible because they believed that, once he was on the throne, peace would return to Benin. They discussed this with Irughe who was in complete agreement. And so the preparations to install the new Oba got under way.

Meanwhile, Ogun continued to wander through the forest, completely unaware, that he had been betrayed by his brother. One day, as he was roaming through the forest, he heard a sound which made him stop dead in his tracks. At first he could not be sure if it was the wind whispering through the leaves and branches, or if it was the tinkle of numerous droplets of water as they hit the rocks below. He moved closer and, as he did so, the sounds became clearer. Soon he found himself staring into a clearing, bordered on one side by the forest and on the other by the river. The music that filtered through his ears was the most beautiful he had ever heard. Simple and yet complicated, sad and yet happy, as cool as an evening breeze and yet as comforting as a familiar room.

Ogun was entranced by the music. He watched from behind a large tree and gasped at what he saw. If the music was beautiful, then the sight that met his eyes could only fill him with wonder and rapture. In the clearing before him, the water maidens were performing a ceremony, presided over by Olokun, the river goddess.

Ogun gasped at the sheer beauty of the water maidens. Young nymphs, dressed in a skin-tight gossamer which showed off their slim, but shapely figures. Never had Ogun seen such grace, such dignity, such fluidity. They danced around Olokun, the goddess of the waters, as they played their instruments.

Ogun was drawn back to his childhood. He remembered the numerous tales the old people had recounted to him about the Nereids, the beautiful yet dangerous spirits of the waters, who were appeased yearly with sacrifices and prayers by the humans who lived within their domain.

As Ogun watched the ceremony, a tranquility descended over him. Suddenly the pain and suffering which had clung to him like a shroud lifted. He was at peace with himself and his surroundings. He forgot the months of suffering he had endured in the forest, he forgot his hunger, he forgot the constant fear of the hunted, he forgot the ache in his limbs. He was in a present that he wished would go on forever. He was taken to a place so beautiful, so serene, that it filled his entire being and lifted him to a plane he had never before experienced.

Then, suddenly, the music stopped. Ogun felt as if he had been brought crashing down to earth. He blinked and it was as if he was seeing everything around him for the first time. There was a newness in the forest. The trees were that much straighter and taller, the leaves that much greener, even the small animals, the squirrels and rabbits who, like him, had

watched the ceremony, seemed to have an extra spring as they bounded back to carry on their business.

The ceremony over, the maidens put down their instruments and walked in a single file behind Olokun into the river. Ogun watched as they disappeared one by one below the surface of the water. Then there was silence, but it was a happy silence, a silence filled with gladness, filled with hope. Somewhere in the back of his mind he still heard the faint echoes of the enchanted music. The goose pimples on his skin slowly faded as did the tingling down his spine.

Regretfully, Ogun was about to go on his way when his eyes were drawn to the musical instruments left unguarded by the banks of the river. An idea came to him. If he took one of the instruments with him as a memento, it would always remind him of this special day.

So Ogun stepped out of his hiding-place and crept up to the edge of the river. There were an assortment of instruments, most very unusual. He studied them for a moment, then reached out and picked up one. It resembled a fife, but was the strangest fife he had ever seen, moulded out of sea-shells. It was the lightest, most delicate instrument he had ever held. He was tempted to put it to his lips, but decided against it. He put it down gently and picked up the next instrument, this one a miniature harp.

As Ogun studied the harp, his hand hit against the strings and they produced a sharp, shrill sound which echoed through the forest. For a moment Ogun was still. He looked around him as the sound died to nothing. Then he noticed a ripple beginning to form on the surface of the river. Realizing the Nereids must be returning, he dropped the harp because it was too large, but picked up the fife, quickly stuffing the instrument into his bag as he stole back into the thick of the forest.

Ogun had not gone far when he heard the rush of several pairs of feet. He looked behind him and saw the water maidens racing after him, swift as the deer of the forest. The anger in their faces was capable of cowering even the hardest of hearts. With a sinking feeling Ogun realized it would be impossible to outrun them. He knew he had to hide. A few yards ahead, there was a thick clump of bush. Ogun slipped behind it and waited with bated breath. His plan worked. He heard the rush of feet as the water maidens rushed past, heading deeper and deeper into the forest. When Ogun could no longer see or hear them, he slipped out of his hiding-place and hurried off in a different direction.

Hours later, Ogun felt safe enough to stop for a rest. He sat underneath a strange, gnarled tree, resting his back on its trunk. He was so exhausted that in a few moments he had fallen fast asleep. When he awoke it was night. The pangs of hunger clutched at his stomach, but a strange sound soon made him forget his discomfort.

Ogun listened and realized that the sounds were coming from the tree. It was weeping, crying and howling pitifully. In between its long howls, it would cry out for someone to relieve it of its pains, to remove the thousands of little worms feeding on its bark and causing it such agony. Ogun listened in silence. At daybreak, he removed his spear from its sheath and carefully picked off every single worm on the tree. When he was satisfied there was not a single worm left, he placed his spear back in its sheath, gathered his belongings and prepared to carry on his journey.

"Wait, good friend," the harsh voice of the tree called out. Ogun stopped. "Who are you?" he asked

"I was once a man like yourself, but I was cursed by a drunken witch to remain in this form forever."

"What can I do?" Ogun asked, concerned.

"You've done all you can, my good friend. I was in agony and you relieved my pain. For that I owe you."

"That's all right. I was glad to help," Ogun replied turning to walk away.

"Wait!" the tree called out, "I want to reward you."

Ogun turned to look at the tree. It was true, he thought - if you looked closely, you could make out in its gnarled, knotted form the beginnings of the shape of a human figure. Two branches on either side which could have been hands joined the thick, contorted trunk. Roughly halfway down, the trunk was split down the middle, and both halves which resembled legs twirled and twisted round each other all the way to the ground. Jutting out of the feet were the roots which sank deep into the earth.

"With what?" asked Ogun curiously.

"Take some bark off my left hand and some off my right hand. Burn it and then ground it into a powder. What you will then have is a powerful magic which will give you anything you desire."

Disbelieving, Ogun did as he was told. When the powder was ready, he decided to test it. Applying it as the tree had instructed, he looked for something to test it on. In a moment of haste, he turned to the tree.

"Destroy yourself so you may never give this power to another," he ordered. He watched, and to his everlasting regret, the tree curled up and died right before his eyes. Ogun realized that what the tree had said to him was true. He put the remainder of the powder in a pouch and placed it in his small sack of possessions. Then he was off once more on his long, lonely journey.

Back in Benin, Irughe was crowned as the Oba of Benin. He chose his brother's name Uwaifiokun, and so became known as Oba Uwaifiokun. There was much rejoicing in the city as everyone hoped that the installation of a new Oba would herald a period of peace and prosperity in the city. But this was not to be.

Uwaifiokun was now the most powerful man in Benin, but his heart was troubled. He knew that somewhere deep in the forest lived the one person he now feared the most - the brother he had betrayed. Uwaifiokun knew that he would not be at peace until Ogun was destroyed. So he confided in a few chiefs and nobles whom he knew were easily corruptible. He bought their silence and loyalty with lavish gifts and huge sums of money. Together they plotted to make sure that Ogun would never return to Benin to claim the throne that was rightfully his.

A band of men were sworn to silence and sent into the forest to track Ogun down and kill him. At the same time, Uwaifiokun jailed or killed anyone who had been a friend of Ogun's. Uwaifiokun was a wicked ruler and struck terror in the hearts of his subjects. The people that had rejoiced at his coronation soon cursed the day he returned unharmed from the forest. Many wished it was Uwaifiokun and not Ogun that had been devoured by wild beasts, for they felt that Ogun would have been a fairer ruler. But no one dared voice such thoughts. To do so was to ask for immediate death.

Several years passed and Benin did not prosper. On the contrary, things got worse and there was widespread hunger and starvation. People were unhappy and scared. The kingdom was more troubled than it had ever been. In fact, things were so bad that a group of worried priests from the palace went to the Oracle to find out why peace and prosperity had not returned to Benin. After all, they said, they had done as the ancestors had demanded and crowned a new Oba.

The reply of the Oracle when it came was truly startling. "No!" the Oracle replied vehemently, "You have not satisfied the ancestors. The rightful heir has yet to accede to the throne."

When Oba Uwaifiokun heard about the visit to the Oracle, he was alarmed. He immediately had the priests killed so they could not spread their message. But already it was too late. The priests had spoken to people who had spoken to others. The word was out that, somewhere, Prince Ogun, the rightful heir, still lived...

In the several years that Prince Ogun had lived in the forests he had become a skilled hunter. He developed a deep understanding of the woods. He knew that, complex as everything seemed on the surface, the forest was really finely balanced with plants and animals depending on each other. He had mastered the art of survival in his surroundings. So it was no coincidence that the numerous search parties, sent into the woods by Oba Uwaifiokun to track Prince Ogun down and kill him, invariably returned back to Benin empty-handed.

One day, Prince Ogun was resting in the branches of a tall iroko tree when he heard voices down below. He sat still and listened.

"It has been two weeks and nothing," said one.

"If we return empty-handed again...I fear the Oba's anger..."

"But no one has been able to find him. If he was still alive, he would have shown himself."

"What kind of man allows his brother to steal his birthright while wandering in the forest like a wild animal?" another sneered.

"A fool who *deserves* to die," said another, shooting into the bushes.

"Come and see what you've killed, Uwa." There was a pause and a rush of feet. Then a satisfied voice said, "This will make a lovely meal."

Prince Ogun watched the men carry away the antelope they had killed. Long after they had gone, he continued to think about what he had heard. It disturbed him deeply, first that anyone should dare to call him a coward, but also the unthinkable. Could it be true that his own younger brother, Irughe, had betrayed him? As night fell over the forest, Prince Ogun reached a decision. He resolved to return to Benin...

The rains had stopped and a hazy dusk was falling over the town. In the market of Ekioba most of the traders had packed up and left for the night, disappointed at their poor sales. An eerie silence had descended on the market. It was broken only by the harsh sounds of a raffia broom dragging on the soggy clay earth. Emotan was always the first to arrive and the last to leave the market, no matter how many or how few her sales. She was a childless old widow and there was no one to rush home to. There were no evening suppers to prepare, no unwashed children to clean and send off to bed. The market was for her an adopted home. She liked to think of the traders as part of her family.

Emotan had just finished sweeping when a stranger stood at her door. "Good evening, Ma," he called.

Emotan turned and looked. The man who stood before her was filthy, dressed completely in rags. He looked so destitute and miserable that she invited him to share her evening meal.

It was only as he was eating that she had a chance to have a good look at the person sitting before her.

"It is you!" she whispered in amazement, "But it can't...yes! It *is* you, Prince Ogun."

"Yes, I am Prince Ogun. I came to you because of the stories I heard about your kindness and generosity. Everywhere, they talk about you. They call you the Queen of Ekioba."

Emotan smiled modestly. "You are too kind." Then a thought dawned on her. "You must be careful, my Prince. Everywhere the Oba, your brother has his spies. They say he wants you dead."

"I know only too well." Prince Ogun replied with a harsh bitter laugh. For a moment he was silent, lost in thought. Then, looking up at Emotan, he said, "I have no right to ask you what I am about to, but I have no choice. I need help. Will you help me, Ma?"

Emotan was gazing at Prince Ogun. He has finally come home, she thought. He will be the one to save us from our wicked ruler. It is as the Oracle predicted.

"Of course, I will help you." she replied simply.

Prince Ogun stayed in Emotan's dwellings until the following evening, during which time she told him what had been happening in Benin. The next day, under the cover of darkness, he prepared to enter the town. His plan was to try and get as many chiefs as possible to support him. The problem was that he had no way of knowing who was loyal to the Oba and who would be loyal to him. After much thinking, he decided to approach Ogiefa Nomuekpo, a powerful chief who had been a friend of his late father, Oba Ohen.

Emotan watched him go and prayed for his safety. Prince Ogun found his way to Ogiefa Nomuekpo's compound. When the old chief was alone, he revealed himself.

"Ogiefa Nomuekpo, it is I, Prince Ogun," he whispered.

The old chief was startled. He stared at Prince Ogun for several moments, eyes wide as if he were looking at a ghost.

"Are you not happy to see me?"

Ogiefa Nomuekpo coughed. "Of course, eh...of course...but it's been seven years, my Prince." He gripped the younger man's shoulders. "They said you had died. Tell me, does anyone know you are here?"

Prince Ogun thought a moment before he replied, "No, I came here first because you were a friend of my father's. I knew if there was a person I could trust, it would be you."

"Yes, yes, of course," the old man agreed, a little too hastily. "It was a very good thing you came here first. We must plan what to do now."

Prince Ogun had no doubts that he had found an ally, especially as, the very next day, Ogiefa Nomuekpo told him that he was setting off to prepare meetings with chiefs who wanted to see the young prince on the throne. Before he went, Ogiefa Nomuekpo warned Prince Ogun about the numerous spies whom the Oba had sent out to search for him. Prince Ogun listened and agreed that it would not be safe to leave Ogiefa Nomuekpo's compound until he returned. But still Ogiefa Nomuekpo seemed worried and distracted.

"What is it?" Prince Ogun asked finally.

"Even here there are spies, in my own household," Ogiefa Nomuekpo replied seriously.

"Perhaps I should find somewhere else to hide till you return?" Prince Ogun suggested.

"No, no, don't do that, it will be too dangerous...I have an idea," Ogiefa Nomuekpo countered.

And that was how Prince Ogun found himself helpless, at the bottom of a dry well. As Ogiefa Nomuekpo pulled up the ladder, he shouted down, "I will soon be back. Don't worry, my Prince."

Prince Ogun watched as the ladder disappeared up the well. Then the top was covered with large leaves, leaving him in partial blackness. Prince Ogun sat on the hard, dry earth, thinking. Already he had waited seven years. A few more hours would not harm him.

Time goes by very slowly when you are sitting in a confined space with nothing to do except daydream. Prince Ogun thought about many things in the hours he was sitting at the bottom of the well, but most of all, he thought about his evil brother. The significance of what he was eventually going to have to do did not escape him. Oba Uwaifiokun had been crowned. In Benin, the only way to remove an Oba was through death. To claim his birthright, he would have to be his own brother's executioner.

A sound from above startled Ogun. He looked up. Someone was pulling aside the leaves.

"Is that you, Ogiefa Nomuekpo?" Ogun called in a loud whisper.

There was no reply. Instead, the face that looked down at him was unfamiliar. Ogun stood up and backed against the wall of the well. Deep lines of worry were etched in his forehead. Could this be one of the spies Ogiefa Nomuekpo had talked about? he wondered.

The face continued to look down at him. Ogun took in the features of a young man. "Did Ogiefa Nomuekpo send you?" he called up.

The young man looked down at Ogun a moment longer. He seemed in no hurry to reply, but, when he finally did, it was to ask, "Is it true you are Prince Ogun?"

Now Ogun knew that the man could not possibly be from Ogiefa Nomuekpo. Ogun realized that, down at the bottom of the well, there was little he could do to defend himself. He decided that, if he must die, he would do so with courage and dignity. So, stretching himself to his full height, he looked up at the stranger and answered: "Yes I am Prince Ogun, son of Oba Ohen."

The face disappeared. As Ogun was wondering what would happen to him, he became aware that the ladder was being lowered. He waited until he could reach it, held on and climbed out of the well. He was prepared to be confronted by a group of soldiers. But the young man who reached down to help him climb out of the well was the only one around.

"Quick, you must go far away from here. My master is not your friend. Even now, he is planning your death."

"Who are you?" Ogun asked, confused.

"I am Edo, one of Ogiefa Nomuekpo's slaves. Do as I say and go. Leave this place or you will die."

Ogun looked at the earnest expression on the young man's face and knew that he spoke the truth.

"Thank you," he said, but the words did not seem enough.

"Go on now," repeated Edo softly and for the first time allowed himself a slight smile.

Ogun turned and ran out of the compound. He walked through the back streets and headed away from the town. Soon he found himself slipping back into the relative sanctuary of the forest.

It was not long before Ogiefa Nomuekpo returned to the well. He was not alone but had with him a group of cronies whom he planned to help him murder Prince Ogun. Edo knew his master only too well. Ogiefa Nomuekpo was as greedy as he was corruptible. When Oba Uwaifiokun had first acceded to the throne, Ogiefa Nomuekpo was one of the first chiefs the frightened monarch had bought. And, since then, handsome sums had secured his continuing loyalty.

As Ogiefa Nomuekpo hurried back to the well that hot afternoon, all he could think about was the money he could demand from the Oba after he had carried out the unpleasant task. He would be rich, beyond his wildest dreams, he thought as he pulled the leaves from the top of the well. He whispered to his men to stay out of sight and called down:

"Prince Ogun, I am back."

When there was no reply, he bent over to peer down into the murky depths.

"Oh, Prince, there is nothing to be afraid of. It is only I, Ogiefa Nomuekpo."

Ogiefa Nomuekpo's eyes began to grow accustomed to the dull light at the bottom of the well. As he gazed down, he realized that there was no one down there.

"Prince Ogun!" he called out sharply, beads of sweat forming on his forehead.

"What is it, sir?" one of his cronies asked, coming forward.

Ogiefa Nomuekpo turned to his men, a look of panic streaked over his face. "He is not there!" he exclaimed uncomprehendingly, as the men came and peered down the well.

"Master, I think it is empty," one remarked, stating the obvious.

But how could he have escaped?" Ogiefa Nomuekpo wondered aloud. "I put him there myself. I took the ladder.

Look, it is exactly where I left it." He pointed to the ladder which lay on the ground by the well.

"Could it be that he has magic?" one of the men ventured.

"Powerful magic," another agreed.

"To disappear just like that, it must be strong," said yet another.

Ogiefa Nomuekpo listened to this exchange in silence. Out of the corner of his eye, he noticed a child hanging around. "Drive that child away," he muttered impatiently.

One of his obedient cronies immediately hurried over to the little boy and was about to shoo him away when the boy told the man something. A few seconds later, the man returned in a highly excitable state. "Master," he called, "Prince Ogun did not disappear. This child saw everything."

Unfortunately, it was true. The child had indeed seen everything. Ogiefa ordered Edo's immediate death for what he termed his act of high treason.

Emotan waited for Prince Ogun to return. When he did not, she realized something must have gone wrong. It did not take her long to decide what she must do. Behind her gentle, grandmotherly facade was a wise old woman. In her many years she had heard much and learned even more. Her aging years had not dulled her mind, but had sharpened it. Emotan knew that Prince Ogun would return and, when he did, she wanted to be ready, to clear the path for him. So, risking her life, she went round the city and talked to those people she knew she could trust. They were people from all walks of life. Some were farmers, others noblemen of royal blood. One thing they all had in common was a deep, undying love for Prince Ogun. Emotan wanted these people to reaffirm to her their support for Prince Ogun. She extracted from them a pledge that, when the time came, they would rise up against their evil Oba and be prepared to lay down their lives for the Prince.

As the days passed and Emotan talked to an ever-increasing number of people, rumours began to filter out. Some of the people she spoke to were not sincere, so they carried the message to disloyal ears. Talk spread of the coming revolution. Soon the word got to the ears of the Oba. He commanded his chiefs to find out who was responsible for the rumours. He also doubled the number of spies in the city and the search parties that combed the forests looking for Prince Ogun.

One night, Emotan was fast asleep in bed when she was awoken by a gentle tap, tap, tapping on her door. Immediately she crept to the door. "Who is it?" she called and, even as she did so, prepared herself for the worst. She knew what she had started. Word was spreading through the city. The Oba's men were hot on the trail, and soon it would lead to her. She had prepared herself for arrest, or even worse. But to her relief it was not the Oba's men who answered but Prince Ogun. This time she was safe.

Emotan threw open her door and embraced the prince with joy. "I had begun to think you would never return," she whispered.

"It's getting more difficult to evade the Oba's men - they seem to be everywhere."

"They are. Come, you must be hungry."

As Emotan gave the prince food she told him of her plan. It would be too dangerous to attack the Oba while he was in the palace. The odds against a successful attack were just too high. As luck would have it, she had heard that in a few days time there was a ceremony to be held in the town. The Oba was expected to walk through the main street during the ceremony. As the Oba only very rarely left the palace, this would be a good time to confront him and kill him.

Prince Ogun listened carefully to everything she said. It made sense. He would confront his brother when he paraded through the streets among the people. Cut him down in his moment of glory. Emotan told him of the support she had mustered for him. "During the ceremony," she said, "those people on your side will hold branches. When you give the signal, they will bring out their weapons and fight for you."

Prince Ogun waited for the day of the ceremony to arrive. During this time he planned and plotted exactly what he would do when the time came. He was unable to meet any of his supporters as things had become so dangerous, but Emotan helped to ferry messages.

The day of the ceremony arrived. By mid afternoon, crowds had already lined the street, even though the Oba's procession was not expected until late afternoon. A handful of people carried branches, but no one bothered to ask them why.

By late afternoon the crowd had grown. Practically the whole of Benin was out on the streets. The sounds of the large drums could be heard in the distance. The procession had begun. The number of people carrying branches had grown to quite a sizeable proportion. As the Oba's procession drew nearer to the centre of town, a man dressed in rags, his face covered with a cloak, slowly inched his way forward. He squeezed past people who, taking one look at him, would move out of his way with distaste. No one bothered to take a closer look. It would have revealed that the tramp was none other than Prince Ogun.

The procession advanced. Soon the onlookers in the city centre could see the dancers who were leading the procession.

They danced slowly and rhythmically, moving forward with every step. Prince Ogun was now in front of the crowd just a few feet from the dancers. He waited.

Soon the dancers had gone past. Now the main part of the procession made its unhurried way forward - sword-bearers, followed by the chiefs and nobles dressed in their resplendent robes. Prince Ogun lowered his face when any of them looked his way. He moved forward, and then suddenly, he saw him. The Oba was at the rear of the main body of the procession. He was dressed beautifully, with dozens of strings of coral beads hanging from his neck and arms. Two chiefs stood on either side of him, supporting his arms as was the custom. His heavy, beaded crown glittered in the setting sun.

Prince Ogun waited a few more moments until the Oba had come even closer. Now he was so close that Prince Ogun could have touched him if he had wanted to. He looked into the bloodshot eyes of his younger brother as he pulled the rags from his own face.

"Uwaifiokun!" he shouted, "Will you not greet the brother you betrayed?"

Uwaifiokun stopped dead in his tracks, his face frozen with shock. A soldier raised his spear, but one of the men loyal to Prince Ogun quickly killed him. Then Oba Uwaifiokun turned as if to try and run, but Prince Ogun removed the magic powder from his pouch. He blew it at his brother and cursed him. In a moment Oba Uwaifiokun fell to the ground stone dead. His crown rolled off his head. Prince Ogun picked it up and lifted it high in the air for all to see. Someone screamed, and then pandemonium broke out. People were rushing about in all directions, some screaming, others crying. There was confusion, there was noise, there was chaos...

For two days and nights fires raged out of control in the city. But eventually peace and order was restored, and Benin belonged to Prince Ogun. He was crowned Oba of Benin and he took the name 'Ewuare', which means, "It is cool at last," or "The trouble is over."

Oba Ewuare is remembered today as "Ewuare the Great." He was a renowned magician, physician, traveller and warrior. He conquered and annexed over 200 towns and villages. In his time, Benin rose in importance and truly became a city.

When Emotan died, Oba Ewuare promised that the memory of her should never be forgotten. He planted a tree at the spot where she used to sit and sell her wares in the market, and he had her deified. Every man invested with a title has to visit this tree, and so must all funeral processions, to pay reverence to the spirit of Emotan, the famous trader and saviour of Oba Ewuare.

The Three Rivals

Part 1

Oba Esigie was a very famous Benin ruler. He came to the throne in 1504 AD. He was the first Benin Oba to learn to read and speak the Portuguese language. Guns were used for the first time in Benin during his reign when he successfully defeated the Attah of Idah. Oba Esigie also had a very famous mother, Queen Idia. She was the first woman in Benin to go to war. But it was a twist of fate which led to Esigie coming to the throne in the first place, for he had two older brothers. Oba Esigie's name before he came to the throne was Osawe. Here is his story...

There once lived three fine young men who were called Ogidogbo, Aruanran and Osawe. They were half-brothers, sons of Ozolua, a powerful and well respected Oba of Benin. The brothers were great rivals. There was nothing they would not argue about. Each was constantly thinking of a way to prove that he was superior to the others in brains, wit or sheer physical strength.

One day, Aruanran came forward with a proposition for his brothers. He challenged them to a test of skill. "Whoever manages to pole-vault over that pond will be declared the strongest," he said.

Osawe looked out at the pond. "But that is madness," he thought, no human being could possibly jump that far. It was with surprise and not a little discomfort that he heard Ogidogbo agree to the challenge. Though Ogidogbo was the eldest of the three, Osawe thought it strange that he constantly felt the need to prove himself.

Osawe was a slight young man, with a sharp, enquiring mind. The first Portuguese visitors to the Kingdom of Benin had recently arrived and, already, Osawe had begun to learn the language. Osawe felt the eyes of his brothers on him. Turning to them, he said, "It is a ridiculous challenge. No one could jump that far."

Aruanran turned to Ogidogbo with a taunting laugh. "I think our brother is scared?" he said.

"That's all right - a coward cannot help but be who he is," Ogidogbo mocked.

Osawe refused to be humiliated by his brothers. Before he could stop himself, he had agreed to take part in the competition.

News of the amazing contest travelled through the Kingdom. On the day of the competition, a crowd had gathered at the pond. The judges were chosen from the ranks of the palace chiefs.

Aruanran had been named Idubor at birth, but he soon received the nickname Aruanran, meaning 'Giant', because of his amazing physical stature. As a young boy, he was already as tall as any man, and as a young man he towered above the tops of trees. Aruanran was proud of his height. He revelled in any activity that gave an opportunity for him to show off his amazing physique and skill.

Aruanran looked out at the large throng of people gathered around the pond. He declared that, as the competition was his idea, he would jump first. Neither Ogidogbo nor Osawe argued with that. In fact, Ogidogbo was worried. The pond was much wider than it had seemed from a distance, *too* wide, in fact. Osawe was determined to delay the moment of *his* jump for as long as possible.

Aruanran picked up his pole and walked to the water's edge. A hush descended on the crowd like a wave, and then excited whispers broke out. The atmosphere was electric. Aruanran stood completely still for a few moments, staring into the calm, blue waters of the pond. His chest was bare. Around his waist was a short, sparkling white cloth. He looked at the crowd, slowly taking them in. The throng throbbed with excitement.

Finally, Aruanran turned with his head held high and walked away from the water's edge. When he judged he had gone far enough, he lifted the pole above his head and waited for quiet. The air of expectancy increased, but then, as if by unspoken general consent, a silence descended on the crowd. A bird which perched in an iroko tree watched the spectacle with interest. It chirped a few times, and then it too fell silent.

Aruanran took a first hesitant step forward, then another, and then another. Soon he was running, cutting through the air, feet thundering on the ground, his soles leaving deep impressions where they landed. Aruanran ran with the grace and majesty of a wild antelope, the ferocity of a lion after its prey, the composure and stealth of a hare. At the edge of the pond, he forced the pole into the ground and allowed himself to be lifted high above the waters. The crowd held its breath as Aruanran thrust himself further and further skyward. Then he let go of the pole and threw his body across the lake.

Aruanran's body hit the baked red earth across the pond. The force of his landing was so great that it left a deep scar in the earth. The crowd watched as Aruanran lay there. They waited, not daring to make a sound. Then, slowly, Aruanran lifted his body from the ground. The crowd went wild. They screamed and cheered. Never before had they seen such an impressive display of physical prowess and skill.

Secretly dismayed, Osawe watched his brother. He had hoped that Aruanran would call off the contest even at the last minute. Up till this moment, he had not believed it possible for anyone to pole-vault across the pond. Now Aruanran had done it, and soon it would be his turn. Already he could see Ogidogbo accepting his pole. He could see the determined look in Ogidogbo's eyes.

A few of the chiefs went up to Ogidogbo to advise him not

to jump. Everyone recognised that Aruanran's challenge was reckless. "Luck more than anything else took him safely across the pond," they said. But Ogidogbo was in no mood to listen to reason. All he could think of was that Aruanran had done it. To give up now was to admit defeat, to be outdone by his younger brother. The shame would be more than he could bear.

Ogidogbo walked a fair distance from the pond. He waited for silence. Then he lifted the pole above his head and began to run. Ogidogbo ran as fast as he could, faster than he ever had before. He reached the water's edge and thrust the pole forcefully into the ground. He could feel himself being lifted into the air, the wind whistling past his ears. He thrust his body forward, legs flailing in the air. The crowd squinted in the sun as they watched. Ogidogbo flew over the pond and landed suddenly with a jarring crunch.

At first, there was simply a sense that something had gone wrong. The crowd waited with bated breath for Ogidogbo to rise. But he did not, and the seconds ticked by. Then someone screamed. Everyone began to talk at once. One, then two attendants rushed over to the unmoving figure. The chiefs left their seats and went to see what was wrong.

From the other side of the pond, Osawe watched the crowd gather round Ogidogbo. He felt the sudden change in the atmosphere and knew that he would not have to jump...

Days later, a bleakness seemed to have descended on the palace. Aruanran and Osawe watched the physicians enter and leave Ogidogbo's private chambers. Eventually it was confirmed: Ogidogbo's fall had done irreparable damage to his legs. There was nothing they could do. He would be lame for the rest of his life.

People gathered from all the four corners of the kingdom to reflect on what the news meant. A lame man could not inherit the throne. In Benin law and custom this was forbidden. That meant that Ogidogbo's claim to the throne passed to his younger brother. Osawe would be the next Oba.

The Three Rivals

Part 2

The rivalry that had existed between Aruanran and Osawe intensified after the pool-jumping incident. Osawe was now being groomed to take over the reins of power on the death of his father, but his claim to the throne was hotly contested.

It was widely known that Aruanran and Osawe were born on the same day. In fact, Aruanran was born a few hours before Osawe, so he was actually the elder of the two. It was an unfortunate twist of fate that led to him being passed over.

Aruanran's mother was a woman called Ohorimi. His was a difficult birth because of his extraordinary size. For the first several hours of his life, he did not make a sound. The midwives doubted that he would live, so they delayed reporting his birth to the Oba. During that time, Osawe was born to Idia. His was a normal delivery. The messengers promptly went to report his birth to the Oba. And so it happened that news of Osawe's birth was received by the Oba before that of Aruanran's. In Benin law, when two births occur on the same day, the first to be reported to the Oba is regarded as the elder.

With the knowledge that he had been robbed of his birthright by the hand of fate, Aruanran left Benin. For several years he wandered around the smaller villages which were part of the kingdom. And the anger in his heart at the knowledge of what he had lost festered like an infected wound. Aruanran's giant stature inspired fear in all those who came across him. He had a bad temper and was quick to punish those who angered him.

It was during his wanderings that Aruanran came across Iyeniroho. A small, wizened woman with a fearful reputation, Iyeniroho was a witch who possessed fantastic, magical powers. She was feared by all who heard of her, except Aruanran.

Aruanran stumbled into her abode and asked the old witch to make up special drugs for him. They were magic potions which Iyeniroho promised would make him invincible to his enemies. Aruanran was determined to use whatever power he could draw from Iyeniroho to defeat and destroy his brother Osawe one day. And so he stayed with Iyeniroho for several months while she made medicines, the like of which she had never made before.

When the potions were ready, Iyeniroho handed them to Aruanran and told him how to use them. Aruanran listened carefully. He had to listen carefully because, though strong and fearless, he was not very clever. Aruanran then gave Iyeniroho the agreed payment, packed his bags and left. The old woman watched the hulking giant leave with a sigh of relief, thinking that was the last she would see of him. She was wrong...

Aruanran had not gone very far when he stopped to think. What if, he wondered, somebody should hear of the old witch's miraculous powers, and that someone should go to her and offer a large sum of money for her to make up the same potions? A greedy old bat like her was hardly likely to refuse. Aruanran became alarmed. He sat down by the side of the road to work out his dilemma. What if, he wondered, that someone with the large sum of money happened to be his brother Osawe? If Iyeniroho was to make the same potions for him, how could he then be destroyed?

Aruanran decided that the risk of the old woman duplicating the potions for someone else was too great. It no longer mattered that she had given her word never to make the same potions for another person. "Never trust an old witch," Aruanran muttered to himself as he rose to his feet. He decided to pay the old woman one last visit.

Iyeniroho was sleeping on a mat in her hut when she became aware that a stranger was on her property. As she rose to investigate, the top of her hut was suddenly torn off. Aruanran's giant stature loomed into the room. Iyeniroho took one look into his great, unblinking eyes and shivered in fear.

Aruanran reached out and picked the old woman up with

one hand. He carried the wriggling, protesting lump as easily as a rag doll. He lifted her clear of the hut and he placed her down on the ground before him.

"How can I trust you?" Aruanran asked as he stared down at the frightened old woman.

"I gave you my word," the old woman whispered.

Aruanran shook his head. With quiet deliberation, he drew his sword and in an instant had sliced off the old woman's head.

"Never trust an old witch," Aruanran muttered to himself as he cleaned his sword and replaced it in its scabbard.

Aruanran continued on his travels. For several years he journeyed on. Sometimes, he would arrive at a town or village which was at war with its neighbour. For shelter and food, Aruanran would offer to help the town defeat its enemy. Afterwards, the grateful people would offer him a house and much wealth, but Aruanran was never interested in staying in one place for very long. He would soon get bored, and that was the signal that it was time to move on.

The years slipped by and then the day finally arrived when Aruanran decided that he was ready to return to Benin.

Oba Ozolua was pleased to see his favourite son return home. He gave Aruanran a special gift of a coral necklace which Aruanran promised would never leave his neck.

Oba Ozolua was aware of the intense hatred brewing between his two sons, so he broke with tradition and made Aruanran the Enogie (or Chief) of Udo, the next biggest town to Benin in the whole of the kingdom. He hoped that this would prevent a civil war between the two brothers after his death. Aruanran therefore left Benin for a second time, to settle at Udo.

Oba Ozolua's last battle was at Ishan. He was fatally wounded by the enemy and he died on the battlefield. As soon as Osawe heard the news, he went off to Ishan to bring his father's body back home for burial in Benin. The news also reached Aruanran. He decided that he wanted the body buried in Udo.

While Osawe was in Ishan making preparations to take the corpse to Benin, he heard that Aruanran was waiting along the Ishan-Benin highway to take possession of their father's body by force. Osawe was troubled at this news. He knew that the only way to Benin was along the Ishan-Benin highway. Even with all his guards he would be no match for his giant brother. Osawe knew that there had to be a way to get the body past Aruanran whom he regarded with deep loathing as a brainless giant. Osawe thought long and hard and then he hit upon a plan.

Osawe ordered two coffins to be made. The first one was constructed of scraps of wood hastily hammered together. It was covered with cowhide and sprinkled with fresh blood. In the hot tropical sun it soon attracted flies which buzzed around the coffin in a most repulsive manner. The coffin was escorted by scantily clad priests. As the coffin was carried slowly down the highway, the priests beat their metal gongs, announcing "Make way, we come to clear the path for our Oba." Everyone who saw the procession believed that the priests were escorting a sacrificial object.

Aruanran and his guards watched this peculiar sight as it made its way towards their roadblock. When the priests reached Aruanran, they stopped and paid their respects. Aruanran gazed at the group standing before him. He crinkled his nose in disgust at the unpleasant smell.

Meanwhile, Aruanran's adviser looked at the coffin with a sneaking suspicion. Turning to Aruanran, he asked curiously, "Baba is this not the corpse of your father?"

Slow-wit that he was, Aruanran was instantly offended that

anyone should dare suggest that his father, the Oba of Benin, would be carried in such an undignified manner. "How dare you!" he exclaimed, turning to his adviser. With a stinging slap to the face, he warned the cowering, now apologetic man never to dare to suggest such rubbish again. Aruanran turned to the cortege and waved it through.

The second coffin Osawe had ordered was of solid brass, lined with red velvet. The chiefs who accompanied the coffin were resplendent in white gowns and red coral beads. Osawe, mounted on a horse, led the procession, which was undeniably grand. In fact, it was so grand that, as soon as Aruanran spotted them from a distance, he felt the hand of victory. Now my little brother will get what is coming to him, he thought as he stepped onto the road and halted the procession.

"Thank you for bringing Baba's body," Aruanran said to Osawe, "You will have to leave it here. I will let you know the

funeral arrangements." He motioned to his guards who stepped forward and removed the coffin. Osawe put up only a nominal show of resistance. He said goodbye to his brother and went on to Benin without the coffin.

Meanwhile, the first procession had reached Benin. The priests announced to the people that the Oba's body had arrived. There was much cheering. The soldiers fired their guns as a mark of respect.

Aruanran and his supporters were still on the Benin-Ishan highway when they heard the gunshots. They were puzzled. Why should the people of Benin be celebrating? they wondered. Aruanran ordered the coffin to be opened. The lid was raised and the men found themselves staring at hundreds of smooth, white pebbles.

Aruanran's anger knew no bounds. The thought that his cheating young brother had tricked him yet again was more than he could bear. The civil war that Oba Ozolua had tried to avert was just about to begin, Aruanran went back to Udo where he immediately began to prepare for war against Benin.

During his travels, Aruanran had met and fallen in love with a woman who gave him a son. He named the child Oni-oni. Aruanran doted on the boy who grew up to be as mischievous as he was handsome. When Aruanran declared war on Benin, Oni-oni was little more than a child, but already he had a fierce fighting spirit. Aruanran was determined that his child should not know the horrors of war until he had reached fighting age, so he left instructions that the boy was not to be allowed out of the house while he was away. Aruanran then gathered his men and went out onto the battlefield.

Aruanran was a formidable warrior. His physical size alone terrified the enemy, and Iyeniroho's medicine made him truly invincible. Aruanran took great satisfaction in seeing the enemy cower before him, below his raised sword. He killed relentlessly, slashing his victims in two with a single swipe of his mighty sword. As the day wore on, the battlefield became a blood-soaked abattoir. The putrid smell of death hung in the air.

Back in Benin, away from the battlefield, reports came to Osawe of the losses inflicted on his army. He was greatly worried - it seemed as if nothing could stop Aruanran.

In Udo, Oni-oni managed to sneak out of the house, past his minders. He found out that his father had gone to war. It annoyed him that he was not told. He and a group of friends broke into Aruanran's shrine, armed themselves and went to the battlefield. Oni-oni started slaying the enemy. His style was like his father's. He tore through the battlefield, cutting down men in their tracks with reckless abandon.

Eventually, Aruanran came upon enemy soldiers who had been killed by hands other than his, but in the same manner. Aruanran looked round the field in anger. Who, he thought, dared to copy him? Aruanran shouted in annoyance. "May this battle kill the person who dares to emulate me."

Not long after, Oni-oni fell on the battlefield, fatally wounded. When Aruanran discovered the body he immediately realized that he had caused his beloved son's death. Aruanran lost all heart for battle. He wandered aimlessly around the battlefield. The enemy took advantage and tried to destroy him, but Iyeniroho's medicine continued to work. Aruanran could not be killed. Numerous slashes to his body seemed to have no effect.

Aruanran continued to wander around the battlefield aimlessly, mourning the death of his only son. Eventually, he came to a river. He stood by the bank for a moment and removed his most precious possession, the coral necklace given to him by Oba Ozolua. He hung it on a branch and cursed anyone who dared wear it, Aruanran then walked into the river and drowned.

Osawe heard what had happened to his brother. Immediately he went to the river to look at the spot where Aruanran had killed himself. Osawe was shown the necklace which was still hanging on a tree where Aruanran had left it. Impulsively, he took the necklace and wore it around his neck, proclaiming victory over Aruanran. Osawe could not know that the necklace had been cursed. As he stood by the river, his generals noticed a startling change come over the young Oba. Osawe began to rant and rave. In an instant he lost his mind and was quite obviously mad. Aruanran's last curse had been fulfilled.

There was instant panic as Osawe's condition became known. News travelled fast and eventually reached his mother Idia who at once set out to help her son. Idia found a physician in Yorubaland who was able to cure Osawe. Later as a mark of gratitude, Osawe made his mother Queen Mother and gave her a palace. Idia became the first Queen Mother of Benin and, to today, she remains the most famous.

The Three Rivals

Part 3

When his father Oba Ozolua was at last buried, as told in the previous story, Osawe was crowned Oba of Benin and he took the name Esigie. For several years, there was peace in the kingdom. But Oba Esigie was young and impetuous. He had not acquired the wisdom and restraint of maturity. His talk was sometimes careless, his actions often reckless.

At this time there was a great chief in the kingdom. His title was Oliha. The Oliha was the leader of the Uzama Nihinron, the seven Councillors of State or kingmakers. They were responsible for installing the Oba into office. The Oliha was so powerful that he had rights and privileges almost similar to the Oba's. In fact, next to the Oba, he was the most important man in the kingdom.

As was usual with all men of importance in those days, the Oliha had several wives. Recently, he had married a beautiful young woman called Imaguero. The Oliha was so infatuated with his new wife that he could not help but talk about her to all who would listen.

One day, Oba Esigie was in the council chamber with the

Oliha and several other chiefs. The Oliha began to talk about his beautiful wife Imaguero. At first everyone listened with customary politeness. Some even teased him mildly. It was all good-natured, but the Oliha continued. He talked about his wonderful wife until everyone present was utterly bored. Several times a chief would try to change the subject, but the Oliha would always twist it round so that he ended up talking about Imaguero.

Esigie hid a yawn behind a fly-switch as the Oliha proudly proclaimed: "My wife is the most faithful woman in the whole of the kingdom - that is why I love her so much." He then stood up, paid his respects to Oba Esigie and left the council chamber.

Esigie thought about what the Oliha had said. He decided there and then to teach him a lesson. The next morning Esigie called one of his most trusted messengers. He gave the messenger some of the most beautiful coral beads he could find. He then told the messenger to go to the Oliha's palace, seek out Imaguero and try and gain entrance to her house by charming her with the beautiful beads.

The messenger went off and, after a few weeks, reported back to Esigie. He had succeeded in getting Imaguero to entertain him in her house.

Esigie was overjoyed. He called a meeting of all the chiefs. Then he sent out a request for the Oliha to attend with Imaguero. When everyone had assembled, Esigie sent a porter to call the messenger. Esigie then asked the Oliha, "What was it you said to me the other day...concerning your young wife?" The Oliha did not have the slightest suspicion that there was anything untoward. He turned to Imaguero and, with a loving smile, announced that she was the most faithful woman in the kingdom.

Benin Folklore

By this time, the messenger had arrived. Esigie ordered him to speak, to tell the assembled audience of what had happened between himself and Imaguero. The messenger cleared his throat and began. He told of how he had gained entrance into the palace, of his meeting with Imaguero. He finished by saying that after he had charmed her with the beads, she was so overjoyed that she entertained him lavishly.

Meanwhile, Imaguero sat beside her husband, rigid with shock. As all eyes turned to her, she knew that the truth was written clearly on her face. Esigie looked on, satisfied that he had proved his point, The Oliha turned to Imaguero, anger and pain etched on his face. The thought that this woman, whom he loved with all his heart, could have succumbed to the charms of a mere messenger was more than he could bear. The dishonour his wife had brought on him tore his heart. In a sudden blinding rage, the Oliha stood up and strangled Imaguero on the spot.

News of Oba Esigie's latest practical joke and how it had ended in tragedy spread through the kingdom. People were of the opinion that Esigie had acted disgracefully.

The Oliha was very bitter at Oba Esigie for the casual way he had destroyed and humiliated him. Daily, the Oliha thought of ways of getting his own back. He did not just want revenge - he wanted to destroy the Oba of Benin.

One day, the Oliha hit upon a plan. He summoned a trusted servant, Aigbovule, and told him to go to the Attah of Idah. "Tell him," the Oliha said, "that the Oba of Benin plans to invade his country. "The Oliha thought a moment longer." Also tell him that if he needs my help to defend his country, I will give it."

When the Attah of Idah heard the news, he was troubled. In those days, Benin was a very powerful and much feared kingdom. It had never lost a battle. The Attah did not doubt the message for one instance. The fact that it came from the second most powerful man in Benin meant that it could not be taken lightly. In consultation with his chiefs, the Attah decided to prepare troops for battle immediately, so he should meet the enemy prepared.

Aigbovule returned to the Oliha with the news that the Attah was preparing his troops for war. The Oliha was pleased - his plan was working. He then sent Aigbovule to Oba Esigie. Aigbovule was instructed to inform the Oba that the Attah of Idah was planning a formidable army to attack and invade Benin. The Oliha then sat back and waited. He hoped that, in the ensuing battle, Oba Esigie would be taken captive and humiliated or killed.

Oba Esigie received news of the planned attack on Benin. He could not understand why the Attah of Idah should mount an unprovoked attack on his city. But intelligence reports reached him that a large army was indeed marching towards Benin. Oba Esigie immediately summoned his war chiefs and instructed them to prepare an army to meet the enemy.

Oba Esigie was not a popular ruler. News of the impending attack on Benin spread through the city, but the men refused to enlist for war. The chiefs reported back to the Oba.

"We cannot form an army," they told the outraged Oba, "the people refuse to fight."

"Kill those who dare disobey their Oba!" exclaimed Esigie haughtily.

"We might as well wait for the Idah troops, Your Majesty," replied the chiefs.

"What do you mean?" fumed the Oba.

"Your Majesty, they *all* refuse to fight," the chiefs replied patiently, "Should we order the death of every Bini man?"

Meanwhile, the Idah troops marched on towards Benin. They reached Udo, a town that must be subdued before they could enter Benin. The people of Udo had prepared for war. They put up a valiant fight against the Idah troops. But the Idahs were the superior army.

Back in Benin, intelligence reports were coming into the city daily about the progress of the Idah troops. Oba Esigie tried everything to get his subjects to prepare for war, from threats to bribes, but nothing worked. The Idah troops finally succeeded in conquering Udo. They began the final march to Benin.

The Oba and his war chiefs spent sleepless nights debating what to do. With no army they could hardly hope to defend the city. As the Idah troops neared Benin, the situation looked increasingly hopeless.

That evening as dusk cast its yellow hue over the city, the atmosphere, though calm, was one of impending doom. The Idah troops were so close to the city that the distant sounds of battle were audible. The Bini men gathered together in small groups, but they still refused to heed the call for war.

An aged priest had watched the contest between the Oba and his people in silence. The old man went into his shrine and took from it the largest and loudest gong he could find. He then prepared to walk through the city streets all night if necessary. He knew that youth is often stubborn, but he could not sit back and allow his people to destroy themselves.

And so the old man walked through the city streets hitting the gong and calling out to all who would listen. He urged the people to fight and defend their city. "The city is your city, the city of our forefathers. It does not belong to Esigie alone. If you do not fight, Esigie will be taken captive, but, when an Oba is captured, is it not true that his subjects also become slaves?

This city of our forefathers does not belong to the Oba alone. We must rise up and defend the land of our ancestors."

The people listened to the old man's words as he slowly made his way through the city. They talked amongst themselves. It made sense. Who are we really punishing by refusing to fight? they asked, "We would be robbing our children of their birthright. We would be giving away the land of our ancestors to foreigners. We cannot allow that to happen."

One man stood up and declared that he would go to war. He entered the Oba's large deserted compound and stood there silently. Then another joined him, and another, and yet another. Then groups of men stood up from where they had gathered and they also entered the Oba's compound. Soon men began to pour into the compound from everywhere in the city. They rushed to join the call for war. The chiefs watched amazed as the compound quickly filled up and men poured out onto the surrounding streets. All were shouting in defiance. "Yes, we will defend our homeland."

The war chiefs now made hurried preparations to defend the city. Led by Oba Esigie, the Binis met the Idah troops on the outskirts of Benin and put up a strong resistance. They fought long and hard, and eventually succeeded in sending the Idah troops into retreat.

One night, when the battle was almost over, the Benin troops set up camp so they could rest before their final assault the following morning. It was a clear, peaceful night. The morale of the men was high - they had chased the Idah troops into retreat and their casualties were relatively light. A full moon had risen high in the sky when an ibis suddenly flew across the face of the moon emitting a high-pitched call. Soon the bird had disappeared, but the men in the camp continued to stare after it. It was almost as if they were frozen into the positions they were in. No one moved. The atmosphere had changed as suddenly as if someone had flicked off a light switch. Oba Esigie, who was sitting with his war generals, realized only too well what was going on in the minds of his men. In Benin, when an ibis flew directly overhead and called out in that manner, it meant bad luck was to follow.

The next morning, the Bini troops refused to go into battle. The generals ordered the men into action, but they just stood there and grumbled amongst themselves. "What is the point?" they said, "We are finished anyway. We will not win this war."

"Nonsense!" cried Oba Esigie, addressing his men, "What if an ibis flew overhead? That does not foretell anything. We are winning the war. To give up now when we are so close to victory will be the worst kind of disaster possible. It will be like snatching defeat from the jaws of the victory."

The troops were not convinced. They refused to listen to

Oba Esigie. Was this not the man who himself had caused the war through his foolhardy ways? Who was he now to tell them anything?

Oba Esigie realized that his troops were not prepared to listen to reason. He ordered his generals to saddle up his horse. He mounted, then turned to the sceptical men watching him curiously. "If you will not give me your support, I will go on alone and face the Idah troops," he declared.

That day on the battlefield, the Bini men saw the man behind the Oba, and it amazed and impressed them all at once. They saw a brave young man full of courage and spirit. They saw a man possessed of dignity and honour. They saw a hero and they were awed.

In an instant, a consensus was reached among the thousands of battle worn men. "Yes, we are men of Benin," they said proudly, "We will fight behind our Oba and, even if we lose the war, it will be a privilege to die in the face of such superior courage."

And so the Benin army followed their Oba. In the ensuing battle, the Idah troops were chased to the banks of the mighty River Niger. It was there that the Attah sent his generals to sue for peace.

After the war was over, Oba Esigie feared to re-enter Benin. He remained at his mother's birthplace and waited to be forgiven by his people. Oba Esigie's subjects respected the courage he had displayed on the battlefield. For that reason they forgave him. A year later, a delegation of chiefs went to bring Oba Esigie back to Benin.

Esigie returned, a much wiser and humbler man. He took up the mantle of office and his reign was long and prosperous.

One of the first things Oba Esigie did on returning to the throne was to order the bronze-casters to cast the ibis on the head of the staffs of office which were normally carried by all chiefs. During ceremonies the chiefs beat the beak of the bird in memory of a brave Oba's decision not to heed the cry of the bird. This is a tradition carried on to the present day.

The King who Refused to Die

Legend has it that long, long ago, in the far recesses of time there lived an old Dieken. A Dieken is a heir to the throne. The Dieken's name was Eghenbuda. Eghenbuda waited many scores of years for his father, the Oba to die. When finally the Oba passed away, leaving the throne for his son, Eghenbuda himself was an old, old man.

And so Eghenbuda assumed the throne of Benin, but he was determined to remain in power for as long as he wished. Old age did not present a problem for him. During the many years that he had been a Dieken with nothing to do, he had become interested in magic. At first, he had merely dabbled, learning about the various cures for ailments and the like. But the passing years found Eghenbuda becoming deeper and deeper involved in the murky secrets of the underworld. Eventually he became a skilled native doctor, able to invoke cures and curses at the flick of a hand. He could strike a man dead with a spell and a few herbs. So great were his powers that he could push away the creeping shadows of death.

Eghenbuda had been on the throne for a few years when he received an odd present from his eldest son, who was now the Dieken. The son had pulled out one of his own grey hairs and

173

placed it in a calabash with four white kolanuts. It was intended to be reminder to Eghenbuda that his son was growing older. Eghenbuda opened the gift and laughed out loud. He thought his son was very witty. Turning to his attendants, he said, "Thank my son for his gift." Then into the same calabash he poured some honey, added two white kolanuts and sent it back to his son.

Eghenbuda's son received the gift from his father with a sinking heart. When he saw the honey, he knew at once what his father was telling him. The life of an Oba was too sweet. Eghenbuda was not ready to go just yet.

Many more years passed. The son was now an old man, weak and frail. Eghenbuda remained on the throne, even though his advanced years dictated that he should have long since returned to the spirit world. He was having too good a time on earth to think of leaving it.

Up in the World of the Unliving, the ancestors watched what was happening in Benin with distaste. Eghenbuda had ignored their persistent reminders that his time on earth was up. The ancestors discussed what they must do and finally decided to send a messenger to tell Eghenbuda that it was time for him to return to the World of the Unliving.

One night, Eghenbuda was asleep when the messenger from the World of the Unliving appeared to him in his dreams.

"Go away," Eghenbuda exclaimed, recognizing the messenger at once, "I will come when I am ready."

But the messenger would not go. He told Eghenbuda that the ancestors were displeased with him for not heeding their calls, and that they demanded he come at once.

Eghenbuda woke up from this dream very much annoyed. He marched into his shrine and muttered some incantations invoking spirits who were loyal to him. He ordered them to get rid of the messenger. And as his loyal spirits chased the messenger back to the World of the Unliving, Eghenbuda shouted after his unwelcome guest, "Tell the ancestors that if I am not coming, what are they going to do about it?" With that he marched back into his chambers.

But Eghenbuda could not sleep. For the next several days he mused over what had happened. Growing increasingly annoyed at what he saw as the impertinence of the ancestors, he decided to pay them a visit. He was determined to face the ancestors and tell them exactly what he thought of them.

So Eghenbuda dressed in his finest robes and went to the World of the Unliving. The ancestors saw him and were annoyed. "This is not how to come to the World of the

Unliving," they told him. "You must return to earth and leave your body behind."

Eghenbuda laughed in the faces of the spirits. "I will come as I choose," he told them.

"You have used up your time on earth. You belong here now," the ancestors said, trying to reason with the stubborn Oba.

"I belong where I choose," he arrogantly replied. "When I am ready, I will give up my place on earth, but not before." He swept up his robes with a grand gesture and turned to leave the World of the Unliving.

"Do not dare disobey your forefathers," the voices of the spirits echoed after him, but Eghenbuda was gone.

The ancestors called a meeting to debate what to do about Eghenbuda. Never before had they been faced with such a problem - a mortal who refused to die. For several days they discussed the problem and finally it was decided that someone would be sent down to earth. His purpose would be to kill Eghenbuda and return his soul to the World of the Unliving. The ancestors agreed that, in the circumstances, it was the only sensible thing to do.

Who would be able to accomplish such a task? the ancestors debated. They agreed that whoever was chosen must be a person who was wily, cunning and brave. Someone who could match Eghenbuda's own remarkable powers.

Word went out in the World of the Unliving that the hunt was on for a person who could kill Eghenbuda and bring his soul to the ancestors. It went without saying that the person who succeeded in carrying out the task would be handsomely rewarded.

Many people applied. From the most obscure parts of the World of the Unliving individuals came requesting to see the ancestors, asking to be allowed to bring back Eghenbuda's soul. Every applicant was carefully vetted because the ancestors did not want to allow just anyone to go down to earth. The Worlds of the Living and the Unliving had been separated from the beginnings of time for a good reason. Many of the inhabitants in the World of the Unliving carried germs which, if let loose on earth, would multiply, causing death, destruction and misery to thousands, and affecting generations yet unborn. The ancestors in their hunt for Eghenbuda's soul had no wish to let loose such havoc on the earth.

The interviews went on for several weeks. During that time, the ancestors listened patiently to the stream of people from all corners of the World of the Unliving who asked to be allowed to go to earth. Many were opportunists with no real ability to conquer the mighty Eghenbuda. Others were more interested in the reward and talked of nothing else. There were those who were bored in the World of the Unliving and wanted to use the opportunity to take a journey somewhere, *anywhere*. And finally there were those who were obviously insane.

At the end of the long selection process, only three candidates remained. The first was a tall old man, bent double by age. He wore a ragged loin-cloth and leaned on a walking-stick. He had a face as rough and lined as a walnut, and where his eyes should have been were two hollow holes. When he talked, his voice echoed as if emitting from a vacant room. His name was Blindness.

Blindness impressed the ancestors with his clear, logical thought and his cunning plan for the removal of Eghenbuda from earth. And so, they gave Blindness the power which would allow him to depart from the World of the Unliving for earth.

Meanwhile, Eghenbuda continued to rule Benin as Oba. His life of luxury and comfort carried on as before. One day, Eghenbuda and his retinue were passing through one of the many hallways in the palace when they walked into what appeared to be a large cobweb. Several minutes were spent by all including Eghenbuda in trying to brush the thin, sticky threads off hands and faces. That was enough time for Blindness to get to work. Silently and invisibly, he crept among them, grabbed hold of the Oba and blew in his face. Eghenbuda felt the hot, dank breath and sensed his sight was leaving him. He cried out in rage knowing what had happened to him was the work of the ancestors. "You will not defeat me," he screamed, "You cannot defeat me."

The now blind Oba ordered his attendants to lead him to his shrine where he invoked his powerful guiding spirits. They came from the shadows and sought out Blindness. In the ensuing battle Blindness was defeated utterly and stripped of his powers. Eghenbuda regained his sight, and banished

Blindness to the far corners of the earth where he still roams alone to this day, spreading his sightlessness throughout the land.

Up in the World of the Unliving the ancestors watched Blindness's unfortunate fate. They decided to call the second of the three selected candidates.

The creature that came before them was terrifyingly ugly - a long slimy thing. This was the father of all snakes. It dragged its massive trunk before the ancestors, leaving a sliver of slime in its wake. The ancestors crinkled their noses in disgust as its foul smell wafted through the room. It stopped its trembling frame before the elders and lifted its head off the ground. With a rasping whisper it greeted the ancestors.

Snake was one of the most feared creatures in the World of the Unliving. Even the ancestors felt uncomfortable in his presence. They gave him the powers to enter earth and waited for him to return with Eghenbuda.

Snake arrived on earth and immediately assumed his disguise, shrinking till he was no more than two feet long. A small and insignificant creature that would hardly draw attention to itself, but through his body flowed the deadliest poison known to man. Snake crawled to the palace to lie in wait for Eghenbuda.

Snake discovered Eghenbuda sitting on his throne. He crept up to the Oba and in a flash had bitten him in the ankle. Eghenbuda felt a sharp nick and immediately withdrew his foot. Snake slunk away to a corner to watch the poison claim its victim.

The poison in Eghenbuda's system began to take effect almost immediately. First the Oba began to sweat. Then his breathing grew irregular as the poison worked its way through his body. Snake watched as the Oba grew weaker by the minute, but Eghenbuda was still defiant. "Look here, Death!" he called out, "Until I want to come, I will not come, so leave me alone! Stop calling me!"

Again Eghenbuda ordered his attendants to carry him to his shrine. He was now too weak to walk. There, he invoked his guardian spirits that once again crept out of the shadows. They searched for Snake and engaged him in battle. The fight was fierce but at the end of the day, the Oba's guardian spirits were triumphant. As soon as Snake was beaten, the poisons he had injected into the Oba's body began to drain away. The cured Eghenbuda ordered Snake to be banished to the furthest reaches of his kingdom where he still dwells today, sending his descendants to destroy unwary people.

From above, the ancestors watched Eghenbuda's defeat of Snake. It was with considerable apprehension that they summoned their third and final selection, Whitlow.

In physical appearance, Whitlow was the smallest and least impressive of the three candidates. In fact, he was the oddest, a small, shapeless mass. He wobbled up to the council elders and bowed low before them. "Your Highnesses, give me the power and I will bring back Eghenbuda's soul."

The ancestors were sceptical. If Blindness, and Snake before him, had failed, how much more likely Whitlow who was merely a third choice and not renowned for anything in particular.

But the ancestors remembered Whitlow must have impressed them sufficiently to merit a place among the three candidates. So they gave him the powers which allowed him to enter earth. As they watched him go, they hoped that, somehow, he would be the one to succeed where the others had failed.

Whitlow arrived on earth and took the form of a speck of

dust. He entered the palace and placed himself on the knob of the door leading into Eghenbuda's private rooms. And there he waited. Soon Eghenbuda arrived to enter his rooms. Unsuspectingly, he reached out and placed a hand on the doorknob. He felt a sharp pain and quickly withdrew his hand. But it was too late. Whitlow had grabbed hold of Eghenbuda's thumb.

Eghenbuda tried everything to destroy Whitlow. He invoked spirits, recited ancient curses, performed sacrifices, but nothing seemed to shake off Whitlow. Days later, the pain in the Oba's right thumb was much worse. In fact, it was so bad that Eghenbuda was unable to sleep. The more tired he got, the worse the pain seemed to be. His medicine men told him that if Whitlow was not destroyed soon, his disease would spread, eventually entering Eghenbuda's bloodstream and killing him.

Eghenbuda was furious. "Why do those useless old spirits refuse to hear when I say that I will come when I am ready!" he ranted.

That night he tossed and turned in his bed. The spasms of pain shooting through his thumb would not stop. Eghenbuda raised the affected thumb and stared at it for a while. It was swollen and throbbing. Was this what would finally destroy him? Would this small, insignificant part of him succeed in bringing down the mighty Eghenbuda who could kill ten thousand men in the battlefield? The mighty Eghenbuda who was feared by men and respected by the spirits? The mighty Eghenbuda who had exposed every secret of the universe? To go like this would not just be humiliating, it would be a great disgrace to the memory of his name.

In a sudden rage, Eghenbuda stood up from his bed and went into the shrine of his forefathers. There he found what he had been looking for. He removed from its resting place the heavy bronze sword. Placing his right hand on the surface of the altar, he raised the sword higher, and higher still. Then with an almighty scream he let the sword descend. In an instant he had sliced off his right thumb.

"You cannot defeat me," Eghenbuda muttered through gritted teeth as the pain of the self-inflicted amputation raced through his body.

Whitlow returned to the World of the Unliving.

"You have failed," said the ancestors.

"Not quite," replied Whitlow, "I brought a piece of him." So saying, he showed them Eghenbuda's right thumb.

Meanwhile, back on earth, Eghenbuda minus a thumb still continued to rule Benin. However, there was one important change. Never again did an Oba of Benin stretch out a hand to open a door. Anytime Eghenbuda or any Oba since wanted a door open, an attendant would be ordered to do it. Up in the World of the Unliving, Whitlow gained respect as the candidate who almost succeeded in defeating the mighty Eghenbuda.

The time finally arrived when Eghenbuda decided that he was ready to die. It was a fine, bright, tropical afternoon when he called his chiefs and told them to accompany him to the place where he had chosen to die. The loyal chiefs and supporters followed Eghenbuda until they arrived at a sea. Eghenbuda made his last speech, saying goodbye to his subjects and reminding them to remember him as the Oba who had chosen when to meet Death and not the other way around.

Then he turned and walked into the sea. Never to be seen again by mortal eyes.